Chocolate Cooking

David Schwartz

TREASURE PRESS

Contents

First published in Great Britain in 1982 by
Octopus Books Ltd

This edition published in 1984 by
Treasure Press
59 Grosvenor Street
London W1

© 1982 Hennerwood Publications Ltd

ISBN 1 85051 004 0

Printed in Hong Kong

INTRODUCTION

Smooth, rich and intense in flavour, chocolate is a luxury enjoyed by everyone. Whether used in simple confectionery, rich puddings or elaborate cakes, it is one of the most versatile ingredients in baking and sweet-making. It is interesting to trace its history from the original form of hard, bitter beans to the confection we know today.

Chocolate and cocoa powder originate from cocoa beans, the seeds of the fruit from a cacao tree. Native to the equatorial regions of the Americas, and now cultivated around the world to within 20 degrees of the Equator, the cacao tree was originally cultivated over 3,000 years ago by the Mayas, Toltecs and Aztecs. They used the beans as currency and to prepare a bitter beverage, mixed with spices, that was at times used as a ceremonial drink.

Columbus brought cocoa beans to Spain after his fourth voyage to the New World, and seventeen years later Cortez and the Spanish Conquistadors were introduced to a chocolate beverage, *xocoatl*, by the Aztecs at the court of the great ruler Montezuma. Described by the Nahuatl words as 'bitter water', *xocoatl* was prepared similarly to the way we process cocoa beans today. After harvesting, the fruit, or cocoa pods, were left to ferment and split open, then the beans and surrounding pulp were removed and left to dry in the sun. The dried, shelled beans were roasted in clay pots and then ground to a paste in a stone mortar, called a *metate*, over a small fire. The paste was mixed with ground spices, then shaped into small cakes or loaves before being dried in the sun. The dried cakes were broken up, melted with hot water and maize (cornmeal), then beaten with a small wooden beater, or *molinet*, until frothy.

Soon after *xocoatl* was introduced to the Spanish court, it was sweetened with sugar and then kept secret for almost a hundred years. It was not until 1606 that the recipe for the beverage was introduced in Italy and it became popular in France in 1660 with the marriage of the Spanish princess, Marie Thérèse, to Louis XIV. In 1657, a Frenchman opened a shop in London selling both the hot chocolate drink, and solid chocolate to be made into the beverage. Chocolate houses, selling the hot drink, soon became popular meeting places throughout Europe. Chocolate remained a luxury item, to be enjoyed by the rich, until the 18th century when chocolate manufacturing began and prices dropped. By 1765 the first chocolate factory in the American colonies was established in New England.

The process for preparing eating chocolate was not developed until the 19th century. In 1828, the Dutchman, C. J. van Houten, founder of the company that still bears his name, patented a process to obtain 'chocolate powder', or cocoa powder as we now know it, by pressing much of the cocoa butter from the ground and roasted beans. Almost twenty years later, the firm of Fry and Sons, of Bristol, combined the extracted cocoa butter with chocolate liquor and sugar to make the first eating chocolate, and, in 1876, Daniel Peter of Switzerland added dried milk to the process to make milk chocolate.

The amount of cocoa butter added to chocolate liquor depends on how the chocolate will be used. Chocolate with a very high proportion of cocoa butter, *couverture*, is a rich-flavoured chocolate with a brittle texture that needs tempering – repeated heating and cooling – to melt and set successfully, and is used only by professional confectioners. For this reason, and for economy, in eating chocolates, which are easier to use for home-baking and sweet making, some of the cocoa butter is replaced by vegetable fat.

Plain chocolate is made with chocolate liquor, cocoa butter and essential vegetable fats, sugar, and flavours – such as vanilla – while in milk chocolate some of the chocolate liquor is replaced with milk solids. Dipping chocolate, which contains a high proportion of vegetable fats, is a good quality soft chocolate for dipped and moulded chocolate confectionery, and is obtainable from trade suppliers, see page 80.

Plain eating chocolate is the type recommended for the recipes throughout the book for its richness in taste and flavour.

The processes described on the next two pages are frequently referred to in the recipes.

Melting chocolate safely

To melt chocolate successfully, put pieces of chocolate in the top of a double boiler, or in a heatproof bowl that will fit securely over a saucepan. Partially fill the pan with water – the water must not touch the bottom of the bowl or the chocolate will overheat and stiffen. Bring the water almost to the boil, remove from the heat, and place the bowl containing the chocolate over the pan. With a spoon, break up the chocolate as it melts, then stir until smooth.

Preparing chocolate for dipping

Put the dipping or plain chocolate in a wide, heatproof bowl over a pan of hot water. Cover the bowl to keep the heat in. Stir the chocolate at intervals until it melts. When all the chocolate has melted (15–20 minutes), uncover and stir until smooth. The chocolate is ready for dipping when it cools to a temperature of 36–43°C/92–110°F.

Chocolate leaves

To make chocolate leaves for cake decoration, first wash and dry fresh leaves with clearly defined veins, such as rose or bay leaves. Melt some chocolate on a heatproof plate over hot water. Holding a leaf by the stem, draw it across the chocolate, so that the leaf is evenly coated but taking care not to spread the chocolate on the other side of the leaf, as this makes peeling difficult. Alternatively, spread the chocolate on to the leaf with a knife. Dry the leaves flat on greaseproof paper, or curved over a rolling pin. When the chocolate is set, carefully peel off each fresh leaf, starting at the stem.

Chocolate curls

Hold a bar of chocolate over the dessert to be decorated and draw the blade of a vegetable peeler along the thin edge of the bar, allowing the curls to fall over the dessert.

Chopped chocolate

Break up some chocolate and with a sharp, heavy knife chop it into coarse or fine pieces.

Grated chocolate

Use a chilled bar of chocolate and grate it as finely or coarsely as desired, on to a plate or work surface.

Chocolate scrolls

Melt some chocolate and, using a flexible palette knife, spread the chocolate to a thickness of about 3 mm/⅛ inch, on a cool work surface. Leave to cool, but not set hard. Push a long firm knife, or metal spatula, at a slight angle, under the chocolate. As you push the knife away from you in a continuous motion, with practice, paper-thin scrolls of chocolate will be formed. Shorter scrolls are formed by pushing the blunt end of a spatula under the chocolate.

Storing chocolate

Store chocolate in a cool, dry place; if you keep it in a refrigerator or freezer, wrap it tightly as it absorbs odour easily. The greyish-white film, or 'bloom', sometimes seen is the result of cocoa butter or sugar crystals rising to the surface after exposure to varying temperatures or excessive moisture. It does not effect the flavour and disappears on melting.

Strong black coffee

To make coffee for a flavouring, triple the amount of ground coffee normally used.

Vanilla sugar

To make your own vanilla sugar, half fill a jar with caster sugar and stand a vanilla pod upright in the sugar. Add more sugar to fill the jar and cover tightly. Leave for two or three weeks before using. As the sugar is used, fill up with more sugar. Replace the vanilla pod after about 6 months.

As a quick substitute, vanilla sugar can be simulated by adding a few drops of vanilla essence to granulated sugar or it can be bought ready made.

Sugar syrups

Sugar syrups are more conveniently tested with an accurate sugar thermometer. To test its accuracy, place the thermometer in a pan of water, bring the water to the boil and the thermometer should register 100°C/212°F. If the thermometer is inaccurate, keep this in mind when calculating the temperature of syrups. A sugar thermometer should never be placed in a hot syrup without being warmed or it will crack. Warm it in hot water first.

The soft-ball stage is cooked to a temperature of 112°–116°C/234°–240°F according to the ingredients of the syrup, but it is advisable to test the consistency as well. Dip the pan of hot syrup in cold water to arrest further cooking. Dip a spoon of syrup into a bowl of iced water, and using your fingertips, gather the syrup into a ball in the water. If the ball just holds its shape, it is at the soft-ball stage.

The short, fine thread stage is cooked to a temperature of 102°C/215°F and is reached when such a thread is spun from the spoon.

Beating egg whites

For best results, fresh eggs at room temperature should be used together with the proper utensils. Free from any trace of yolk, the whites should be beaten with a balloon whisk in a large, clean bowl, dry and free from fat, made of glass, porcelain or stainless steel rather than plastic. Copper bowls, however, produce the best results; the chemical reaction between the metal and egg white produces a more stable foam but to prevent discolouring, the egg white should be used within 15 minutes. Although electric mixers save time and effort the result is less satisfactory than if the whites are whisked by hand.

Storing egg yolks and egg whites

Surplus egg yolks and egg whites can be stored tightly covered in the refrigerator. Egg yolks, although best used immediately, will keep for a day or two, while egg whites can be stored for 4 to 5 days or frozen, but should be at room temperature before beating.

Unsalted butter

Unsalted butter is recommended throughout for its creamy richness of flavour. With lightly salted or salted butter, the taste is disappointingly flat.

Liquid glucose

This is used in a small number of recipes. It is obtainable from the chemist's.

CAKES

Chocolate cakes can be served as a simple accompaniment to afternoon tea or coffee or as an elegant showpiece to conclude a dinner. The recipes require time and care but patience is well rewarded by the results. The cakes are finished with different chocolate decorations described in the introduction and filled and iced with various types of creams. The simplest of these is a flavoured whipped cream for which double or whipping cream can be used and the most involved is a butter cream, a rich mixture made by whisking hot sugar syrup into egg yolks and then blending this with beaten butter. Buttercream is best used straightaway, however it can be stored in the refrigerator covered with cling film or foil for a day or two.

Black and white pound cake

Metric	Imperial
65 g plain chocolate, broken into pieces	2½ oz plain chocolate, broken into pieces
50 ml strong black coffee	2 fl oz strong black coffee
225 g unsalted butter	8 oz unsalted butter
225 g sugar	8 oz sugar
5 eggs	5 eggs
225 g plain flour, sifted	8 oz plain flour, sifted
1 × 1.25 ml spoon vanilla essence	¼ teaspoon vanilla essence
good pinch of baking soda	good pinch of baking soda

Preparation time: 25 minutes
Cooking time: about 1¼–1½ hours
Oven: 180°C, 350°F, Gas Mark 4

Melt the chocolate with the coffee in a small saucepan over a low heat, stirring continuously until smooth. Remove from the heat and leave to cool, stirring occasionally.
Butter and dust a 20 cm/8 inch spring-form cake tin with flour, using the base with the central funnel. Beat the butter in a mixing bowl, until pale and soft. Add the sugar and beat until light and fluffy. Add the eggs, 1 at a time, beating well after each addition. Sift the flour into the bowl and gently fold into the egg mixture until just incorporated. Remove half of the batter to a mixing bowl, stir the vanilla essence into it and spoon into the tin. Smooth the surface of the batter with a spatula.
Stir the chocolate and baking soda into the remaining mixture and pour evenly over the vanilla batter. Run a knife once through the batter to create a streaked effect when the cake is baked. Level the top and bake in a preheated oven for 1–1¼ hours.
Remove from the oven and leave the cake in the tin on a wire tray to cool completely.
Makes one 20 cm/8 inch cake

Black and white pound cake; Devil's food cake

Devil's food cake

Metric	Imperial
75 g plain chocolate, broken into pieces	3 oz plain chocolate, broken into pieces
175 ml strong black coffee	6 fl oz strong black coffee
175 g unsalted butter	6 oz unsalted butter
225 g soft dark brown sugar	8 oz soft dark brown sugar
50 g vanilla sugar	2 oz vanilla sugar
3 eggs	3 eggs
275 g plain flour	10 oz plain flour
1½ × 5 ml spoons bicarbonate of soda	1½ teaspoons bicarbonate of soda
175 ml soured cream	6 fl oz soured cream

Icing:	Icing:
450 g sugar	1 lb sugar
300 ml water	½ pint water
2 egg whites, stiffly beaten	2 egg whites, stiffly beaten

Preparation time: 35 minutes
Cooking time: 45–50 minutes
Oven: 190°C, 375°F, Gas Mark 5

Place the chocolate in a saucepan with the coffee, stir over a low heat until the chocolate melts and the mixture is smooth. Leave to cool. Butter and line three 20 cm/8 inch sandwich tins with greaseproof paper. Brush the paper with melted butter and dust with flour. Beat the butter in a mixing bowl, until pale and soft. Add the sugars and beat until fluffy. Add the eggs, 1 at a time, beating well after each addition. Stir in the chocolate. Sift the flour and bicarbonate of soda together on to a sheet of greaseproof paper and fold into the chocolate mixture alternating, in 2 or 3 additions, with the soured cream.
Divide the mixture between the tins and bake in a preheated oven for 25 minutes or until a skewer inserted into the centre comes out clean. Remove from the oven and leave in the tins on a wire tray for 5 minutes before turning out to cool completely.
To make the icing, place the sugar and water in a heavy saucepan and stir over a medium heat until the sugar dissolves. Brush away any sugar crystals that have formed on the sides of the pan with a pastry brush dipped in cold water. Increase the heat and bring to the boil. Cook to the soft-ball stage, 115°C/238°F. Remove from the heat and dip the base in cold water to arrest further cooking. Gradually whisk the syrup into the beaten egg whites. Continue beating until the icing thickens and loses its sheen. Spread immediately between the cake layers and over the top and sides.
Makes one 3-layer 20 cm/8 inch cake

Chocolate variety

Metric	Imperial
4 eggs, separated, whites stiffly beaten	4 eggs, separated, whites stiffly beaten
75 g sugar	3 oz sugar
40 g vanilla sugar	1½ oz vanilla sugar
40 g plain flour, sifted	1½ oz plain flour, sifted
40 g ground almonds	1½ oz ground almonds
20 g cocoa powder	¾ oz cocoa powder

Butter cream:

Metric	Imperial
100 g sugar	4 oz sugar
100 ml water	3½ fl oz water
5 egg yolks	5 egg yolks
225 g unsalted butter	8 oz unsalted butter
25 g Praline Powder (page 44)	1 oz Praline Powder (page 44)
25 g plain chocolate, melted	1 oz plain chocolate, melted
1 × 15 ml spoon strong black coffee	1 tablespoon strong black coffee

To decorate:

Metric	Imperial
grated chocolate	grated chocolate
icing sugar	icing sugar

Preparation time: 45 minutes
Cooking time: 45–50 minutes
Oven: 180°C, 350°F, Gas Mark 4

Butter and line two 18 cm/7 inch round cake tins with greaseproof paper. Brush the paper with melted butter and dust with flour. Whisk the egg yolks with the sugars in a mixing bowl, until the mixture falls off the whisk in a thick ribbon. Sift the flour, almonds and cocoa powder on to a sheet of greaseproof paper. Gently fold in a third of the flour mixture, a third of the beaten egg whites and repeat until all of the flour mixture and egg whites are incorporated.

Pour the mixture into the tins and bake in a preheated oven for 25 minutes. Remove from the oven and leave the cakes in the tins for 5 minutes, before turning them out to cool completely.

To make the butter cream, follow the method described in the Dobostorte, page 23, omitting the melted chocolate. Divide the cream between 4 bowls. Stir the praline powder into 1 bowl, the melted chocolate into the second, the coffee into the third and reserve the last.

To assemble the cake, slice each sponge into 2 layers. Spread the bottom layer with the chocolate butter cream, the next layer with the coffee-flavoured butter cream and the third layer with the praline-flavoured butter cream, cover with the final layer and spread the reserved butter cream on top. Sprinkle with grated chocolate dusted with icing sugar.

Makes one 4-layer 18 cm/7 inch cake

Chocolate pound cake

Metric	Imperial
225 g sugar	8 oz sugar
65 ml water	2½ fl oz water
65 g cocoa powder	2½ oz cocoa powder
225 g unsalted butter	8 oz unsalted butter
225 g caster sugar	8 oz caster sugar
5 eggs, separated, whites stiffly beaten	5 eggs, separated, whites stiffly beaten
225 g plain flour, sifted	8 oz plain flour, sifted
1 × 1.25 ml spoon bicarbonate of soda	¼ teaspoon bicarbonate of soda
pinch of salt	pinch of salt
icing sugar	icing sugar

Preparation time: 35 minutes
Cooking time: about 1½ hours
Oven: 160°C, 325°F, Gas Mark 3

Pound cakes are best left overnight before slicing and well-wrapped will keep up to a week.

Dissolve the sugar with the water in a heavy saucepan, stirring constantly over a medium heat. Bring to the boil and cook the syrup to 102°C/215°F, or until the syrup spins a short, fine thread from a spoon. Remove the pan from the heat and dip its base in cold water to arrest further cooking. Add the cocoa powder and stir until smooth. Leave to cool.

Butter and line a 1 kg/2 lb loaf tin with greaseproof paper. Brush the paper with melted butter and dust with flour. Beat the butter in a mixing bowl, until pale and smooth. Add the sugar and beat until light and fluffy. Add the egg yolks, 1 at a time, beating well after each addition. Stir in the chocolate syrup.

Sift the flour, bicarbonate of soda and salt together into the bowl and fold into the chocolate mixture. Gently fold in a third of the beaten egg whites, then fold in the rest.

Pour the mixture into the tin and bake in a preheated oven for 1¼ hours or until a skewer inserted into the centre comes out clean. Remove to a wire tray and leave the cake in the tin for 10 minutes before turning it out to cool completely. When cool, remove the lining paper. Dust with icing sugar before serving.

Makes one 1 kg/2 lb cake

From the front: Chocolate pound cake; Chocolate variety

Orange chocolate layer cake

Metric
150 g unsalted butter, softened
grated rind of ½ orange
225 g caster sugar
5 eggs, separated, whites stiffly beaten
150 g plain chocolate, melted
150 g plain flour, sifted
4 medium oranges
450 g sugar
450 ml water

Orange butter cream:
75 g sugar
85 ml water
3 egg yolks (sizes 1, 2)
grated rind of ½ orange
175 g unsalted butter

To decorate:
chocolate scrolls
icing sugar

Imperial
5 oz unsalted butter, softened
grated rind of ½ orange
8 oz caster sugar
5 eggs, separated, whites stiffly beaten
5 oz plain chocolate, melted
5 oz plain flour, sifted
4 medium oranges
1 lb sugar
¾ pint water

Orange butter cream:
3 oz sugar
3 fl oz water
3 egg yolks (sizes 1, 2)
grated rind of ½ orange
6 oz unsalted butter

To decorate:
chocolate scrolls
icing sugar

Preparation time: 1¾ hours, plus cooling
Cooking time: 1 hour 20 minutes
Oven: 180°C, 350°F, Gas Mark 4

This layer cake with its fresh orange filling is just right for a special occasion.

Butter and line a 20 cm/8 inch round cake tin with greaseproof paper. Brush the paper with melted butter and dust with flour. Beat the butter together with the orange rind in a mixing bowl, until pale and soft. Add the sugar and beat until light and fluffy. Add the egg yolks, 1 at a time, beating well after each addition. Stir in the melted chocolate. Sift the flour into the bowl and fold into the butter mixture. Fold in a third of the beaten egg whites, then fold in the rest. Pour the mixture into the tin and bake in a preheated oven for 50–60 minutes or until a skewer inserted into the centre comes out clean. Remove from the oven and leave the cake in the tin for 5–10 minutes before turning it out to cool completely.

Cut the rind and pith from the oranges and then segment them, reserving the juice. Place the sugar and water in a saucepan and stir over a low heat until the sugar is dissolved. Cook the mixture to 102°C/215°F or until the syrup spins a short, fine thread from a spoon. Add the orange segments and reserved juice and poach for 3–5 minutes. Strain the syrup into another pan, cook until reduced by half and reserve. To make the butter cream, dissolve the sugar with the water in a heavy saucepan. Cook the syrup over a medium heat to a temperature of 102°C/215°F. Whisk the egg yolks with the orange rind in a bowl, until thick and creamy. Slowly pour the hot syrup over the yolks, beating constantly until the mixture is cool and fluffy. In another bowl, beat the butter until it is smooth and creamy. Add the egg yolk mixture a little at a time, beating constantly until the butter cream is firm and shiny.

To assemble the cake, slice the sponge into 2 layers. Brush the bottom layer, cut side up, with some of the reserved syrup. Spread it with a layer of the butter cream and arrange the orange segments on top. Add the top layer and brush the upper side with more syrup. Spread the remainder of the butter cream over the top and sides of the cake. Decorate with the chocolate scrolls dusted with icing sugar.
Makes one 2-layer 20 cm/8 inch cake

Chocolate Swiss roll with truffles

Metric
butter, melted, for
  greasing
4 eggs, separated, whites
  stiffly beaten
100 g sugar
50 g plain flour, sifted
40 g cocoa powder, sifted
caster sugar

Chocolate filling:
175 ml double cream
1 × 15 ml spoon rum
150 g plain chocolate,
  broken into pieces
75 g grated chocolate
5 Truffles (page 72), to
  decorate

Imperial
butter, melted, for
  greasing
4 eggs, separated, whites
  stiffly beaten
4 oz sugar
2 oz plain flour, sifted
1 ½ oz cocoa powder, sifted
caster sugar

Chocolate filling:
6 fl oz double cream
1 tablespoon rum
5 oz plain chocolate,
  broken into pieces
3 oz grated chocolate
5 Truffles (page 72), to
  decorate

Preparation time: 40 minutes, plus chilling
Cooking time: 20–25 minutes
Oven: 230°C, 450°F, Gas Mark 8

Butter and line a 23 × 33 cm/9 × 13 inch Swiss roll tin with greaseproof paper. Brush the paper with melted butter and dust with flour. Whisk the egg yolks with the sugar in a mixing bowl until the mixture falls off the whisk in a thick ribbon. Sift the flour together with the cocoa powder on to a sheet of greaseproof paper. Gently fold in a third of the flour mixture, then a third of the beaten egg whites and repeat until all the flour and egg whites are incorporated. Pour the mixture into the tin, smooth the surface, and bake in a preheated oven for 10–12 minutes, or until the cake is springy to the touch.

Spread a kitchen towel on a work surface, cover it with greaseproof paper and sprinkle the paper with caster sugar. When cooked, turn the sponge out upside down on to the sugared paper. Peel off the grease-proof paper used to line the tin.

Trim the edges of the sponge and make a shallow groove along a short side of the cake 2.5 cm/1 inch from the edge. Cover the sponge with greaseproof paper. Fold the sponge over at the groove. Using the towel to support the cake, roll up the sponge and cover with a damp cloth until cool.

To prepare the chocolate filling, bring the cream and rum just to the boil in a heavy saucepan. Stir in the broken chocolate and continue stirring as the choco-late melts until the mixture is thick and smooth. Chill the mixture until firm, at least 1 hour, then vigor-ously whisk the chocolate until light and fluffy.

Unroll the sponge and remove the greaseproof paper. Spread the sponge with a layer of the chocolate filling and roll it up. Spread the remaining mixture neatly over first the top of the cake, before gently rolling the cake in the grated chocolate, then over the sides of the cake, gently pressing in the grated chocolate. Leave to set in a cool place. Decorate the cake with truffles. Makes one 23 cm/9 inch cake.

Orange chocolate layer cake;
Chocolate Swiss roll with truffles

Chocolate Mont Blanc

Preparation time: 15 minutes
Cooking time: 55 minutes
Oven: 180°C, 350°F, Gas Mark 4

Metric
225 g plain chocolate,
  broken into pieces
1 × 15 ml spoon rum
1 × 15 ml spoon strong
  black coffee
100 g unsalted butter, cut
  into pieces
4 eggs, separated, whites
  stiffly beaten
100 g sugar
75 g plain flour
300 ml double cream

Imperial
8 oz plain chocolate,
  broken into pieces
1 tablespoon rum
1 tablespoon strong
  black coffee
4 oz unsalted butter, cut
  into pieces
4 eggs, separated, whites
  stiffly beaten
4 oz sugar
3 oz plain flour
½ pint double cream

Butter and flour a Kugelhopf mould. Melt the chocolate together with the rum and coffee in a heat-proof bowl over a saucepan of gently simmering water. Stir until the chocolate melts and the mixture is smooth. Remove from the heat and stir in the butter pieces. When the butter has melted, stir in the egg yolks, the sugar and then the flour. Gently fold in a third of the beaten egg whites and then the rest.
Pour the mixture into the mould and bake in a pre-heated oven for 45 minutes or until the cake is springy to the touch.
Remove from the oven and leave the cake in the mould on a wire tray for 5 minutes before turning it out to cool completely.
Whisk the cream in a mixing bowl until light and fluffy, barely holding soft peaks. Spoon the cream into the centre of the cake allowing it to flow down the sides.
Serves 6

Chocolate Mont Blanc; Chocolate meringue layer cake

Chocolate meringue layer cake

Preparation time: 1 hour
Cooking time: 2–2¼ hours
Oven: 160°C, 325°F, Gas Mark 3;
180°C, 350°F, Gas Mark 4

Metric
75 g ground walnuts
1 × 15 ml spoon cocoa
powder, sifted
120 g caster sugar
3 egg whites, stiffly
beaten

Imperial
3 oz ground walnuts
1 tablespoon cocoa
powder, sifted
4 ½ oz caster sugar
3 egg whites, stiffly
beaten

Sponge:
50 g plain flour, sifted
45 g cocoa powder, sifted
4 eggs (sizes 1, 2),
separated, whites
stiffly beaten
120 g sugar

Sponge:
2 oz plain flour, sifted
1 ¾ oz cocoa powder, sifted
4 eggs (sizes 1, 2),
separated, whites
stiffly beaten
4 ½ oz sugar

Filling:
600 ml double or whipping
cream
2 × 15 ml spoons cocoa
powder
65 g vanilla sugar

Filling:
1 pt double or whipping
cream
2 tablespoons cocoa
powder
2 ½ oz vanilla sugar

To decorate:
chopped walnuts
chocolate scrolls
icing sugar

To decorate:
chopped walnuts
chocolate scrolls
icing sugar

Line 2 baking sheets with greaseproof paper, securing each corner with a dot of butter and, using a cake tin as a guide, pencil an 18 cm/7 inch circle on each tray. Combine the walnuts, cocoa powder and 50 g/2 oz of the sugar in a bowl. Beat in the remainder of the sugar into the beaten egg whites, a little at a time, and whisk until stiff. Gently fold the walnut and sugar mixture into the beaten egg whites.

Spoon the meringue into a piping bag fitted with a 1 cm/½ inch plain nozzle. Pipe a spiral of the meringue on each of the baking sheets. Bake the meringue in a preheated oven for 1½ hours or until crisp. Remove from the oven and allow the meringue to cool on the trays. Carefully peel away the paper from the bottom of each meringue.

Butter and line an 18 cm/7 inch spring-form cake tin with greaseproof paper. Brush the paper with melted butter and dust with flour. Sift the flour together with the cocoa powder on to a sheet of greaseproof paper. Whisk the egg yolks with the sugar in a mixing bowl, until the mixture falls off the whisk in a thick ribbon. Gently fold in a third of the flour mixture, then a third of the egg whites and repeat until all of the flour and egg whites are incorporated. Pour the mixture into the tin and bake in a preheated oven at the higher temperature for 40–45 minutes or until the cake is springy to the touch.

Remove from the oven and leave the cake in the tin on a wire tray for 5 minutes before turning it out to cool completely. To make the filling, whisk together the cream, cocoa powder and vanilla sugar in a mixing bowl, until the mixture forms light, soft peaks.

To assemble the cake, slice the sponge into 2 layers. Spread a layer of meringue with a layer of the whipped cream. Cover with alternate layers of sponge, cream and meringue. Spread the remaining cream over the top and sides of the cake. Decorate the sides of the cake with chopped walnuts and the top with the chocolate scrolls. Sift a small amount of icing sugar over the scrolls.

Makes one 4-layer 18 cm/7 inch cake

Chocolate angel food

Metric
25 g plain flour, sifted
25 g cocoa powder, sifted
120 g caster sugar
5 egg whites
pinch of salt
1 × 2.5 ml spoon cream
    of tartar
icing sugar
Chocolate Ice Cream
    (page 64) or whipped
    cream, to serve

Imperial
1 oz plain flour, sifted
1 oz cocoa powder, sifted
4½ oz caster sugar
5 egg whites
pinch of salt
½ teaspoon cream of
    tartar
icing sugar
Chocolate Ice Cream
    (page 64) or whipped
    cream, to serve

Preparation time: 20 minutes
Cooking time: 30–40 minutes
Oven: 180°C, 350°F, Gas Mark 4

This feather-light cake requires gentle handling but is easy to make.

Dust, but do not butter, an 18 cm/7 inch spring-form cake tin with flour, using the base with the central funnel. Sift the flour, cocoa powder and 75 g/3 oz of the sugar together 3 times.
Whisk the egg whites with the salt in a mixing bowl until foamy and add the cream of tartar. Continue whisking until the egg whites form stiff peaks. Add the remaining sugar, beating until the egg whites are firm and glossy.
Sift the flour mixture over the egg whites and gently, but thoroughly, fold into the egg whites. Pour the mixture immediately into the tin. Bake in a preheated oven for 30–40 minutes or until a skewer comes out clean and the cake is springy to the touch.
Remove from the oven and invert the tin on to a wire tray. Leave the cake to cool completely. Run a knife around the sides and unmould from the tin. Dust with icing sugar. Serve sliced with chocolate ice cream or whipped cream.
Makes one 25 cm/10 inch cake

Mousse cake

Metric
120 g plain chocolate,
  broken into pieces
50 ml milk
2 eggs, separated, whites
  stiffly beaten

Sponge:
butter, melted, for
  greasing
6 eggs
175 g sugar
100 g plain flour, sifted
25 g ground almonds

To finish:
275 ml double cream
1 × 15 ml spoon vanilla
  sugar

To decorate:
75 g flaked almonds,
  roasted
chocolate scrolls
icing sugar

Imperial
4 ½ oz plain chocolate,
  broken into pieces
2 fl oz milk
2 eggs, separated, whites
  stiffly beaten

Sponge:
butter, melted, for
  greasing
6 eggs
6 oz sugar
4 oz plain flour, sifted
1 oz ground almonds

To finish:
9 fl oz double cream
1 tablespoon vanilla
  sugar

To decorate:
3 oz flaked almonds,
  roasted
chocolate scrolls
icing sugar

Preparation time: 55 minutes, plus chilling overnight
Cooking time: 55–60 minutes
Oven: 180°C, 350°F, Gas Mark 4

The mousse for this cake is prepared one day in advance. It is a delicious cake, worth taking time over for a special occasion. When assembled, the cake is best eaten immediately.

To make the chocolate mousse, stir the chocolate with the milk in a saucepan over low heat, until the chocolate melts and the mixture is smooth. Remove from the heat and beat in the egg yolks, 1 at a time, stirring constantly until the mixture is smooth and glossy. Fold a third of the beaten egg whites into the chocolate, then fold in the rest. Chill the mousse overnight.
Butter and line a 20 cm/8 inch round cake tin with greaseproof paper. Brush the paper with melted butter and dust with flour. Whisk the eggs and sugar lightly together in a mixing bowl. Place the bowl over a pan of gently simmering water and whisk the mixture until lukewarm. Remove the pan from the heat and, without removing the bowl, continue to whisk the mixture until it triples in bulk and falls off the whisk in a thick ribbon. Sift together the flour and almonds and gently fold into the mixture in 3 additions, until just blended.
Pour the mixture into the tin and bake in a preheated oven for 35–40 minutes or until the cake is springy to the touch.
Remove from the oven and leave the cake in the tin on a wire tray for 5 minutes before turning it out to cool completely.
Meanwhile, whisk together the cream and vanilla sugar in a mixing bowl, until the mixture forms light, firm peaks.
To assemble the cake, slice the sponge into 3 layers. Spread the bottom layer of the cake with half of the chocolate mousse, cover with a layer of cake and spread it with a thick layer of the whipped cream. Place the third layer of the cake on top and cover it with the remaining chocolate mousse. Spread the remaining whipped cream around the sides of the cake, gently pressing in the roasted almonds. Arrange the chocolate scrolls on top and lightly dust with icing sugar. Chill until ready to serve.
Makes one 3-layer 20 cm/8 inch cake

Chocolate angel food; Mousse cake

Chocolate butterfly cakes

Metric	Imperial
100 g unsalted butter, softened	4 oz unsalted butter, softened
100 g caster sugar	4 oz caster sugar
2 eggs, separated, whites stiffly beaten	2 eggs, separated, whites stiffly beaten
75 g plain flour	3 oz plain flour
25 g cocoa powder	1 oz cocoa powder
1 × 2.5 ml spoon baking powder	½ teaspoon baking powder
pinch of salt	pinch of salt
75 g raspberries	3 oz raspberries
caster sugar	caster sugar
175 ml double cream	6 fl oz double cream

Preparation time: 45 minutes, plus cooling
Cooking time: 20–25 minutes
Oven: 180°C, 350°F, Gas Mark 4

Line a 12-form patty tin with paper cases. Beat the butter in a mixing bowl, until pale and soft. Add the sugar and beat until light and fluffy. Add the egg yolks, 1 at a time, beating well after each addition. Sift together the flour, cocoa powder, baking powder and salt into the mixing bowl. Fold into the butter mixture. Gently fold in a third of the beaten egg whites, then fold in the rest.

Divide the mixture evenly between the paper cases and bake in a preheated oven for 20–25 minutes or until a skewer inserted into the centre comes out clean. Remove to a wire tray and leave to cool in a tin for 2–3 minutes before turning out to cool completely.

Starting 5 mm/¼ inch in from the edge, remove the top of each cake by cutting in and down slightly to form a bowl-shaped cavity. Reserve the tops.

Set aside 12 raspberries and purée the remainder through a nylon sieve. Sweeten to taste with sugar. Whip the cream with the purée until it forms peaks. Using a piping bag fitted with a star nozzle, fill the cavity of each cake with most of the whipped cream mixture. Cut each reserved cake top in half. Place each half, cut side outwards, into the whipped cream at a slight angle. Pipe a rosette of whipped cream in the centre and top with a reserved raspberry.
Makes 12

Chocolate butterfly cakes; Triple chocolate cake

Triple chocolate cake

Preparation time: 40 minutes, plus cooling
Cooking time: 45–55 minutes
Oven: 180°C, 350°F, Gas Mark 4

Metric
3 eggs, separated, whites
   stiffly beaten
75 g sugar
50 g plain chocolate,
   melted
75 g plain flour

**Chocolate butter
cream:**
50 g sugar
50 ml water
2 egg yolks (sizes 1, 2)
150 g unsalted butter
40 g plain chocolate,
   melted

Chocolate icing:
65 ml double cream
1 × 15 ml spoon strong
   black coffee
65 g plain chocolate,
   broken into pieces

Imperial
3 eggs, separated, whites
   stiffly beaten
3 oz sugar
2 oz plain chocolate,
   melted
3 oz plain flour

**Chocolate butter
cream:**
2 oz sugar
2 fl oz water
2 egg yolks (sizes 1, 2)
5 oz unsalted butter
1½ oz plain chocolate,
   melted

Chocolate icing:
2½ fl oz double cream
1 tablespoon strong black
   coffee
2½ oz plain chocolate,
   broken into pieces

Butter and line a 15 cm/6 inch spring-form cake tin with greaseproof paper. Brush the paper with melted butter and dust with flour. Whisk the egg yolks with the sugar in a mixing bowl until the mixture falls off the whisk in a thick ribbon. Fold in the melted chocolate. Gently fold in a third of the flour, then a third of the beaten egg whites and repeat until all of the flour and egg whites are incorporated.

Pour the mixture into the tin and bake in a preheated oven for 30–40 minutes or until the cake is springy to the touch.

Remove from the oven and leave the cake in the tin on a wire tray for 5 minutes before turning it out to cool completely.

To make the chocolate butter cream, dissolve the sugar with the water in a heavy saucepan. Brush away any sugar crystals that have formed on the sides of the pan with a pastry brush dipped in cold water. Cook the syrup over medium heat to a temperature of 102°C/215°F or until the syrup spins a short fine thread from the spoon. Whisk the egg yolks in a bowl until thick and creamy. Slowly pour the hot syrup over the egg yolks, beating constantly until the mixture is cool and fluffy.

In another bowl, beat the butter until smooth and creamy. Add the egg yolk mixture, a little at a time, and continue beating until the butter cream is firm and shiny. Stir in the melted chocolate.

To assemble the cake, slice the sponge into 3 layers and spread the butter cream between each layer. Reassemble the cake.

To make the icing, pour the cream and coffee into a saucepan and bring just to the boil. Stir in the broken chocolate and continue stirring as the chocolate melts, until the mixture becomes cool, thick and smooth. When thick, pour the icing over the cake and leave to set for about 15 minutes.

Makes one 3-layer 15 cm/6 inch cake

Variation:
For a more elaborate presentation, decorate the cake with chocolate leaves and piped butter cream.

Chocolate cherry cake

Preparation time: 35–40 minutes
Cooking time: about 1½ hours
Oven: 180°C, 350°F, Gas Mark 4

Metric
7 eggs, separated, whites
   stiffly beaten
200 g sugar
75 g plain flour, sifted
75 g cocoa powder
40 g unsalted butter,
   melted and cooled

Imperial
7 eggs, separated, whites
   stiffly beaten
7 oz sugar
3 oz plain flour, sifted
3 oz cocoa powder
1½ oz unsalted butter,
   melted and cooled

Filling:
175 ml double cream
2 × 15 ml spoons brandy
175 g plain chocolate,
   broken into pieces
450 g sugar
300 ml water
450 g cherries, stoned

Filling:
6 fl oz double cream
2 tablespoons brandy
6 oz plain chocolate,
   broken into pieces
1 lb sugar
½ pint water
1 lb cherries, stoned

Icing:
175 ml double cream
1 × 15 ml spoon brandy
175 g plain chocolate,
   broken into pieces

Icing:
6 fl oz double cream
1 tablespoon brandy
6 oz plain chocolate,
   broken into pieces

To decorate:
chocolate scrolls
icing sugar

To decorate:
chocolate scrolls
icing sugar

An exotic cake combining the rich taste of chocolate and brandy with the refreshing flavour of cherries.

Butter and line a 23 cm/9 inch round cake tin with greaseproof paper. Brush the paper with melted butter and dust with flour. Whisk the egg yolks with the sugar in a mixing bowl, until the mixture falls off the whisk in a thick ribbon.

Sift the flour and cocoa powder together on to a sheet of greaseproof paper. Gently fold into the egg yolk mixture a third of the flour mixture, a third of the egg whites, then a third of the butter and repeat until all of the ingredients are incorporated. Pour the mixture into the tin and bake in a preheated oven for 50–60 minutes or until the cake is springy to the touch. Remove from the oven and leave the cake in the tin on a wire tray for 5 minutes before turning it out to cool completely.

To make the filling, bring the cream just to the boil in a heavy saucepan. Add the 1 × 15 ml spoon/1 tablespoon of the brandy and the chocolate pieces, stirring continuously until the chocolate melts and the mixture is thick and smooth. Leave to chill for at least 1 hour. Place the sugar and water in a heavy saucepan and stir over low heat, until the sugar is dissolved. Bring to the boil and cook the syrup to 102°C/215°F or until the syrup spins a short, fine thread from a spoon. Add the cherries and poach for 5–7 minutes. Strain the syrup into another pan and boil to reduce by half. Stir in the remaining brandy and reserve.

When the chilled chocolate is firm, whisk until light and fluffy. Slice the sponge into 2 layers, brush the bottom layer, cut side up, with some of the reserved syrup. Spread it with a layer of the chocolate and arrange the poached cherries on top, reserving some for decoration. Add the top layer and brush the upper side with more syrup. Spread the chocolate mixture over the top of the cake, reserving some for decoration. Chill the cake until the chocolate is firm.

To make the icing, bring the cream just to the boil in a saucepan. Add the brandy and chocolate pieces, stirring continuously until the chocolate melts and the mixture is thick and smooth. Remove from the heat and leave until lukewarm, stirring occasionally. Pour quickly over the cake. Allow to set.

Pipe the remaining whisked chocolate around the cake and decorate with the chocolate scrolls and reserved cherries. Lightly dust the top with sifted icing sugar.

Makes one 2-layer 23 cm/9 inch cake

Variation:
When fresh cherries are not available, use tinned cherries, reserving their liquid and adding it to the brandy. Tinned cherries do not need to be poached.

Chocolate cherry cake

Chocolate potato cake

Preparation time: 55 minutes, plus cooling
Cooking time: 30 minutes
Oven: 190°C, 375°F, Gas Mark 5

Metric
100 g hot mashed potato
2 × 15 ml spoons double
   cream
65 g unsalted butter,
   softened
200 g sugar
50 g plain chocolate,
   melted
¾ × 5 ml spoon
   bicarbonate of soda
2 × 15 ml spoons water
3 eggs, separated, yolks
   beaten until light,
   whites stiffly beaten
100 g plain flour
1 × 5 ml spoon baking
   powder
1 × 1.25 ml spoon salt
50 ml milk
½ × 15 ml spoon rum

Imperial
4 oz hot mashed potato
2 tablespoons double
   cream
2½ oz unsalted butter,
   softened
7 oz sugar
2 oz plain chocolate,
   melted
¾ teaspoon bicarbonate
   of soda
2 tablespoons water
3 eggs, separated, yolks
   beaten until light,
   whites stiffly beaten
4 oz plain flour
1 teaspoon baking
   powder
¼ teaspoon salt
2 fl oz milk
½ tablespoon rum

Rum-cocoa icing:
40 g unsalted butter
225 g icing sugar
2 × 15 ml spoons cocoa
   powder
1 × 1.25 ml spoon salt
1 × 15 ml spoon rum
1½ × 15 ml spoon strong
   black coffee

Rum-cocoa icing:
1½ oz unsalted butter
8 oz icing sugar
2 tablespoons cocoa
   powder
¼ teaspoon salt
1 tablespoon rum
1½ tablespoons strong
   black coffee

The unlikely combination of mashed potato and chocolate makes a light and moist cake with the rum adding a richness of flavour.

Butter and line two 18 cm/7 inch round cake tins with greaseproof paper. Brush the paper with melted butter and dust with flour. Combine the mashed potato with the cream in a heatproof bowl. Keep hot over a pan of hot water.
Beat the butter in a mixing bowl, until pale and soft. Add the sugar and beat until well mixed. Add the creamed potato and melted chocolate. Dissolve the bicarbonate of soda in the water and add to the butter mixture. Beat in the egg yolks 1 at a time. Sift the flour, baking powder and salt together twice. Fold them into the batter, adding alternately with the milk and rum. Gently fold in a third of the egg whites, then fold in the rest.
Divide the mixture between the tins and bake in a preheated oven for 30 minutes or until a skewer inserted into the centre comes out clean. Remove from the oven and leave the cakes in the tins on a wire tray for 5 minutes before turning them out to cool completely.
To make the icing, beat the butter until pale and soft. Sift together the icing sugar, cocoa powder and salt and gradually incorporate into the butter. Stir in the rum and coffee. Spread a layer of icing between the 2 layers and over the top and sides of the cake.
Makes one 2-layer 18 cm/7 inch cake

Dobostorte

Metric
6 eggs, separated, whites
   stiffly beaten
grated rind of 1 lemon
175 g sugar
150 g plain flour, sifted

**Chocolate butter
cream:**
100 g sugar
100 ml water
5 egg yolks
225 g unsalted butter
100 g plain chocolate,
   melted

Caramel glaze:
150 g sugar
lemon juice

Imperial
6 eggs, separated, whites
   stiffly beaten
grated rind of 1 lemon
6 oz sugar
5 oz plain flour, sifted

**Chocolate butter
cream:**
4 oz sugar
3 ½ fl oz water
5 egg yolks
8 oz unsalted butter
4 oz plain chocolate,
   melted

Caramel glaze:
5 oz sugar
lemon juice

Preparation time: 35 minutes
Cooking time: 40–45 minutes
Oven: 200°C, 400°F, Gas Mark 6

This is a 7 layer cake. If you do not have 7 cake tins, divide the sponge mixture into 7, then use as many tins as you have and cook in batches.

Butter and line seven 20 cm/8 inch round cake tins with greaseproof paper. Brush the paper with melted butter and dust with flour. Whisk the egg yolks with the lemon rind and sugar in a mixing bowl, until the mixture falls off the whisk in a thick ribbon. Gently fold in a third of the flour, then a third of the beaten egg whites and repeat until all of the flour and egg whites are incorporated. Divide the mixture between the tins and bake in 2 batches, in a preheated oven for 8–10 minutes each. Remove from the oven and turn out on to wire trays to cool.

To make the butter cream, dissolve the sugar with the water in a heavy saucepan. Bring to the boil and cook the syrup over a medium heat to 102°C/215°F or until the syrup spins a short, fine thread from a spoon. Whisk the egg yolks in a bowl, until thick and creamy. Slowly pour the hot syrup over the egg yolks, beating constantly until the mixture is cool and fluffy.

In another bowl, beat the butter until it is smooth and creamy. Add the egg yolk mixture, a little at a time, and continue beating until the butter cream is firm and shiny. Stir in the melted chocolate.

Spread 6 of the 7 cake layers with a layer of the chocolate butter cream and sandwich together.

To make the caramel glaze, put the sugar with a few drops of lemon juice into a heavy saucepan and cook over a low heat, stirring constantly. Continue stirring until all the sugar is dissolved and the caramel is clear and just brown. Pour immediately over the remaining cake layer. Before the caramel sets, cut the cake layer, with a knife dipped in hot water, into 8 equal wedges. Carefully place the wedges on top of the cake with a blob of butter cream under one corner of each to lift them and spread the remaining butter cream around the sides.

Makes one 7-layer 20 cm/8 inch cake

Chocolate potato cake; Dobostorte

Chocolate cheesecake

Metric
65 g plain flour, sifted
25 g ground walnuts
25 g vanilla sugar
pinch of salt
25 g unsalted butter, cut
 into pieces
1–2 × 5 ml spoons cold
 water

Filling:
450 g full fat soft cheese
150 g sugar
2 × 15 ml spoons plain
 flour
3 eggs, separated, whites
 stiffly beaten
85 g plain chocolate,
 melted
85 ml double cream

To decorate:
chocolate scrolls
icing sugar

Imperial
2½ oz plain flour, sifted
1 oz ground walnuts
1 oz vanilla sugar
pinch of salt
1 oz unsalted butter, cut
 into pieces
1–2 teaspoons cold
 water

Filling:
1 lb full fat soft cheese
5 oz sugar
2 tablespoons plain
 flour
3 eggs, separated, whites
 stiffly beaten
3½ oz plain chocolate,
 melted
3 fl oz double cream

To decorate:
chocolate scrolls
icing sugar

Preparation time: 25 minutes, plus chilling overnight
Cooking time: 1¼ hours
Oven: 200°C, 400°F, Gas Mark 6
 160°C, 325°F, Gas Mark 3

To make the pastry, sift the flour, walnuts, sugar and salt into a large mixing bowl. Add the butter and using your fingertips, rub into the mixture until it resembles coarse breadcrumbs. Add enough water to make a workable dough and gather the dough into a ball. Wrap in cling film or foil and chill for 1 hour.
Butter the base of a 20 cm/8 inch round spring-form tin. Place the dough on top and roll out to cover. Trim the edges. Bake in a preheated oven for 15 minutes or until golden.
Remove from the oven and leave to cool over a wire tray. When cool, butter the ring and lock it on to the base. Beat the cheese in a mixing bowl, until soft and fluffy. Add the sugar and flour and mix well. Beat in the egg yolks, 1 at a time, beating well after each addition. Stir in the melted chocolate and cream. Gently fold in a third of the beaten egg whites, then fold in the rest. Pour the mixture into the tin and bake in a preheated oven for 1 hour or until the filling is firm to the touch.
Remove from the oven to a wire tray. Leave for at least 2 hours before removing the sides of the tin and transferring to a serving platter. Decorate with chocolate scrolls and dust lightly with sifted icing sugar. Chill overnight before serving.
Makes one 20 cm/8 inch cake

Marbled cheesecake

Metric
1 quantity Rich
 Shortcrust Pastry
 (page 40)

Cheese filling:
450 g full fat soft cheese
2 × 15 ml spoons plain
 flour
200 g vanilla sugar
grated rind of ½ orange
2 eggs
2 egg yolks
2½ × 15 ml spoons double
 cream
25 g plain chocolate,
 melted
2 × 5 ml spoons brandy

Imperial
1 quantity Rich
 Shortcrust Pastry
 (page 40)

Cheese filling:
1 lb full fat soft cheese
2 tablespoons plain
 flour
7 oz vanilla sugar
grated rind of ½ orange
2 eggs
2 egg yolks
2½ tablespoons double
 cream
1 oz plain chocolate,
 melted
2 teaspoons brandy

Preparation time: 45 minutes, plus overnight chilling
Cooking time: 1¼–1½ hours
Oven: 200°C, 400°F, Gas Mark 6;
 230°C, 450°F, Gas Mark 8;
 110°C, 225°F, Gas Mark ¼

Shape the pastry into a ball, wrap it in cling film or foil and chill for 1 hour.
Butter the base of an 18 cm/7 inch round spring-form tin. Halve the pastry and roll out 1 half to cover the base. Trim the edges. Bake in a preheated oven for 15 minutes or until golden.
Remove from the oven and leave to cool on a wire tray. When cool, butter the sides of the spring-form tin and lock on to the base. Roll out the remaining dough into 2 equal strips, 8 cm/3 inches wide to fit the inside of the ring. Fix the strips inside the ring and gently press the edges to seal on to the base. Trim the edges and chill while preparing the filling.
Beat the cheese in a mixing bowl, until soft and fluffy. Add the flour, sugar and grated orange rind and mix well. Beat in the eggs, 1 at a time, followed by the egg yolks. Stir in the cream. Remove a third of the batter to another mixing bowl and stir the melted chocolate and brandy into it.
Pour the vanilla-flavoured filling into the pastry shell. Add spoonfuls of the chocolate filling on top to create a marbled effect. Bake in a preheated oven for 15 minutes. Reduce the heat and bake for 50–65 minutes or until the filling is firm to the touch.
Remove from the oven to a wire tray. Leave for at least 2 hours before removing the sides of the spring-form tin. Chill overnight before serving.
Serves 6

From the left: Chocolate cheesecake;
Chocolate spice cake; Marbled cheesecake

Chocolate spice cake

Preparation time: 25 minutes
Cooking time: 40–50 minutes
Oven: 180°C, 350°F, Gas Mark 4

Metric
5 eggs, separated, whites
   stiffly beaten
175 g sugar
75 g plain chocolate,
   melted
75 g plain flour
1 × 2.5 ml spoon ground
   cinnamon
1 × 2.5 ml spoon ground
   cloves
1 × 2.5 ml spoon ground
   nutmeg

Cinnamon topping:
ground cinnamon
icing sugar

Imperial
5 eggs, separated, whites
   stiffly beaten
6 oz sugar
3 oz plain chocolate,
   melted
3 oz plain flour
½ teaspoon ground
   cinnamon
½ teaspoon ground
   cloves
½ teaspoon ground
   nutmeg

Cinnamon topping:
ground cinnamon
icing sugar

Butter and line a 20 cm/8 inch spring-form cake tin with greaseproof paper, using the base with the central funnel. Brush the paper with melted butter and dust with flour. Beat the egg yolks with the sugar in a mixing bowl, until the mixture falls off the whisk in a thick ribbon. Stir in the melted chocolate. Sift the flour, cinnamon, cloves and nutmeg together into the mixing bowl and gently fold into the batter mixture. Gently fold in a third of the beaten egg whites, then fold in the rest.

Pour the mixture into the tin and bake in a preheated oven for 40–50 minutes, or until a skewer inserted into the centre of the cake comes out clean. Remove from the oven and leave the cake in the tin on a wire tray for 10 minutes before turning it out to cool completely. Dust the surface of the cake with a little icing sugar and/or ground cinnamon.

Makes one 20 cm/8 inch cake

Truffle torte

Metric
100 g unsalted butter,
   softened
100 g caster sugar
3 eggs, separated, whites
   stiffly beaten
100 g plain chocolate,
   melted
25 g plain flour
150 g ground hazelnuts

Chocolate icing:
150 ml double cream
150 g plain chocolate,
   broken into pieces
8 Chocolate Spirals (page
   75), to decorate

Imperial
4 oz unsalted butter,
   softened
4 oz caster sugar
3 eggs, separated, whites
   stiffly beaten
4 oz plain chocolate,
   melted
1 oz plain flour
5 oz ground hazelnuts

Chocolate icing:
¼ pint double cream
5 oz plain chocolate,
   broken into pieces
8 Chocolate Spirals (page
   75), to decorate

Preparation time: 1 hour
Cooking time: about 1¼ hours
Oven: 180°C, 350°F, Gas Mark 4

Butter and line an 18 cm/7 inch spring-form cake tin with greaseproof paper. Brush the paper with melted butter and dust with flour.

Beat the butter in a mixing bowl, until pale and soft. Add the sugar and beat until light and fluffy. Add the egg yolks, 1 at a time, beating well after each addition. Stir in the melted chocolate. Sift together the flour and hazelnuts and then sift again into the mixing bowl. Fold into the butter mixture. Gently fold in a third of the beaten egg whites, then fold in the rest.

Pour the mixture into the prepared tin and bake in a preheated oven for 55–60 minutes or until firm and springy to the touch.

Remove from the oven and leave the cake in the tin on a wire tray for 5 minutes before turning it out to cool completely.

To make the icing, place the cream in a saucepan and bring just to the boil. Add the chocolate, stirring until the chocolate melts and the mixture is thick and smooth. Pour the mixture evenly over the cake; before the chocolate sets, decorate with 8 chocolate spirals. Makes one 18 cm/7 inch cake

Yule log

Preparation time: 45 minutes
Cooking time: 25–30 minutes
Oven: 230°C, 450°F, Gas Mark 8

Metric
4 eggs, separated, whites
  stiffly beaten
75 g sugar
25 g vanilla sugar
90 g plain flour, sifted
caster sugar

Chocolate butter cream:
75 g sugar
85 ml water
4 egg yolks
175 g unsalted butter
50 g plain chocolate,
  melted
½ × 15 ml spoon rum

Imperial
4 eggs, separated, whites
  stiffly beaten
3 oz sugar
1 oz vanilla sugar
3½ oz plain flour, sifted
caster sugar

Chocolate butter cream:
3 oz sugar
3 fl oz water
4 egg yolks
6 oz unsalted butter
2 oz plain chocolate,
  melted
½ tablespoon rum

Butter and line a 23 × 33 cm/9 × 13 inch Swiss roll tin with greaseproof paper. Brush the paper with melted butter and dust with flour. Whisk the egg yolks with the sugars in a mixing bowl, until the mixture falls off the whisk in a thick ribbon. Gently fold in a third of the flour, then a third of the beaten egg whites and repeat until all the flour and egg whites are incorporated. Pour the mixture into the tin, smooth the surface, and bake in a preheated oven for 10–12 minutes or until golden brown.

Spread a kitchen towel on a work surface, cover it with greaseproof paper and sprinkle the paper with caster sugar. When cooked, turn the sponge out upside down on to the sugared paper. Peel off the greaseproof paper used to line the tin.

Trim the edges of the sponge and make a shallow groove along a short side of the cake 2.5 cm/1 inch from the edge. Cover the sponge with greaseproof paper. Fold the sponge over at the groove. Using the towel to support the cake, roll up the sponge and cover with a damp cloth until cool.

To make the butter cream, dissolve the sugar in the water in a heavy saucepan. Bring to the boil and cook the syrup over a medium heat to a temperature of 102°C/215°F, or until the syrup spins a short, fine thread from a spoon. Whisk the egg yolks in a bowl, until thick and creamy. Slowly pour the hot syrup over the egg yolks, beating constantly until the mixture is cool and fluffy.

In another bowl, beat the butter until smooth and creamy. Add the egg yolk mixture, a little at a time, and continue beating until the butter cream is firm and shiny. Stir in the melted chocolate and rum.

Unroll the sponge and remove the greaseproof paper. Spread the sponge with a layer of chocolate butter cream and roll it up. Spread a layer of butter cream on both ends. Spoon the remaining butter cream into a piping bag fitted with a 1–2 cm/½–¾ inch star nozzle. Pipe the butter cream along the length of the cake to resemble the bark. Leave to set in a cool place.

Variation:
For more festive occasions, the yule log can be further decorated with chocolate leaves and/or small meringue mushrooms (page 74).
Makes one 23 cm/9 inch cake

Truffle torte; Yule log

Sachertorte

Metric	Imperial
165 g unsalted butter, softened	5 ½ oz unsalted butter, softened
165 g sugar	5 ½ oz sugar
7 eggs, separated, whites stiffly beaten	7 eggs, separated, whites stiffly beaten
165 g plain chocolate, melted	5 ½ oz plain chocolate, melted
100 g plain flour, sieved,	4 oz plain flour, sieved
40 g ground almonds	1 ½ oz ground almonds
100 g apricot jam	4 oz apricot jam

Chocolate icing:	Chocolate icing:
100 ml double cream	3 ½ fl oz double cream
2 × 5 ml spoons brandy	2 teaspoons brandy
100 g plain chocolate, broken into pieces	4 oz plain chocolate, broken into pieces
chocolate leaves, to decorate	chocolate leaves, to decorate
icing sugar, for dusting	icing sugar, for dusting

Preparation time: 40 minutes, plus cooling
Cooking time: about 1¼ hours
Oven: 180°C, 350°F, Gas Mark 4

This is one of Vienna's most famous cakes, renowned for its lightness, which is achieved by the high proportion of egg whites.

Butter and line an 18 cm/7 inch round cake tin with greaseproof paper. Brush the paper with melted butter and dust with flour.
Beat the butter in a mixing bowl, until pale and soft. Add the sugar and beat until light and fluffy. Add the egg yolks, 1 at a time, beating well after each addition. Stir in the melted chocolate. Sift the flour and almonds into the bowl and fold into the butter mixture. Gently fold in a third of the beaten egg whites, then fold in the rest.
Pour the mixture into the tin and bake in a preheated oven for 45–55 minutes or until a skewer inserted into the centre comes out clean. Remove from the oven and leave the cake in the tin for 10 minutes before turning it out to cool completely. Warm the apricot jam and spread it over the top and sides of the cake. Leave it to set.
To make the icing, place the cream in a saucepan with the brandy and bring just to the boil. Add the chocolate pieces and stir until the chocolate melts and is thick and smooth. Pour the chocolate mixture evenly over the cake and leave to set, about 15 minutes. Decorate with chocolate leaves, dusted with icing sugar.
Makes one 18 cm/7 inch cake

Dark raspberry cake; Sachertorte

Dark raspberry cake

Metric	Imperial
6 eggs, separated, whites stiffly beaten	6 eggs, separated, whites stiffly beaten
100 g sugar	4 oz sugar
50 g vanilla sugar	2 oz vanilla sugar
65 g plain flour, sifted	2 ½ oz plain flour, sifted
65 g cocoa powder	2 ½ oz cocoa powder

Filling:	Filling:
450 ml double cream	¾ pint double cream
50 g vanilla sugar	2 oz vanilla sugar
65 ml rum or Kirsch	2 ½ fl oz rum or Kirsch
75 g redcurrant jelly	3 oz redcurrant jelly
225 g raspberries	½ lb raspberries
225 g strawberries, halved	½ lb strawberries, halved
To decorate:	**To decorate:**
chocolate scrolls (optional)	chocolate scrolls (optional)
icing sugar	icing sugar

Preparation time: 45 minutes
Cooking time: 40–45 minutes
Oven: 180°C, 350°F, Gas Mark 4

Butter and line a 20 cm/8 inch round cake tin with greaseproof paper. Brush the paper with melted butter and dust with flour. Whisk the egg yolks with the sugars in a mixing bowl until the mixture falls off the whisk in a thick ribbon. Sift the flour and cocoa powder together on to a sheet of greaseproof paper. Gently fold in a third of the flour mixture, then a third of the beaten egg whites and repeat until all of the flour and egg whites are incorporated.
Pour the mixture into the tin and bake in a preheated oven for 30–40 minutes or until the cake is springy to the touch. Remove from the oven and leave the cake in the tin on a wire tray for 5 minutes before turning it out to cool completely.
Whisk together the cream and vanilla sugar in a mixing bowl, until the mixture forms light, firm peaks. To assemble the cake, slice the sponge into 3 layers. Warm 1½ × 15 ml spoons/1½ tablespoons of the rum or Kirsch together with the redcurrant jelly in a small saucepan, stirring constantly, until the mixture forms a syrup. Brush the warm syrup over the bottom layer, arrange the raspberries on top and spread over a layer of the whipped cream. Cover with another layer of the cake, brush with the remaining rum or Kirsch. Arrange the strawberries on top and spread over a thick layer of the whipped cream. Place the third layer of cake on top and spread the top with the whipped cream. Decorate with a piped border of the remaining whipped cream and chocolate scrolls (if using) dusted with icing sugar.
Makes one 3-layer 20 cm/8 inch cake

PIES AND PASTRIES

Pastry combines well with chocolate to provide a
variety of tastes and textures. Rich shortcrust,
puff and choux pastry are used in several of the
recipes and there is a recipe for strudel pastry,
as well as for an almond and egg white pastry
as the base for crackling pie. Rich shortcrust
pastry is best chilled before use. It can be patched
if it cracks when being handled.

Mille-feuilles au chocolat

Metric
flour, for dusting
1 quantity Puff Pastry
    (page 36)
100 ml double cream
25 g vanilla sugar
½ quantity Chocolate
    Pastry Cream
    (page 35)
25 g icing sugar

Imperial
flour, for dusting
1 quantity Puff Pastry
    (page 36)
3 ½ fl oz double cream
1 oz vanilla sugar
½ quantity Chocolate
    Pastry Cream
    (page 35)
1 oz icing sugar

Preparation time: 1¼ hours
Cooking time: 20 minutes
Oven: 220°C, 425°F, Gas Mark 7

Lightly flour a work surface and roll out the puff pastry 3 mm/⅛ inch thick and trim into a rectangle 23 × 38 cm/9 × 15 inches. Cut into 3 equal rectangles, place on a baking sheet and prick with a fork. Chill for 30 minutes.
Bake the dough in a preheated oven for 20 minutes or until well puffed and golden-brown. Remove to a wire tray to cool. When cool, trim the edges of the pastry with a knife.
Lightly whip the cream with the sugar and fold into the chocolate pastry cream. Spread half the cream on to 1 layer of the pastry. Cover with another layer and spread this with the rest of the cream. Place the third rectangle on top and sift the icing sugar over it.
For a special effect, heat a skewer until red hot, then lay it across the top of the pastry in diagonal lines.
Makes one 13 × 23 cm/5 × 9 inch pastry

Mille-feuilles au chocolat; Chocolate cream pie

Chocolate cream pie

Metric
1 quantity Rich
    Shortcrust Pastry
    (page 40)

Imperial
1 quantity Rich
    Shortcrust Pastry
    (page 40)

Filling:
1 quantity Chocolate
    Pastry Cream (page
    35), warmed

Filling:
1 quantity Chocolate
    Pastry Cream (page
    35), warmed

Topping:
5 egg whites
185 g caster sugar

Topping:
5 egg whites
6 ½ oz caster sugar

Preparation time: 35 minutes, plus cooling
Cooking time: 40–50 minutes
Oven: 230°C, 450°F, Gas Mark 8

On a floured work surface, roll the pastry out to a thickness of 3–5 mm/⅛–¼ inch and use to line a 23 cm/9 inch fluted pie tin, 4 cm/1½ inches deep. Cover with greaseproof paper weighted with beans or rice and bake blind in a preheated oven for 15 minutes until the edges are lightly coloured. Remove the paper and weights and bake for another 15 minutes or until the base is lightly coloured. Remove to a wire tray and leave to cool before removing the tin.
When cool, pour the chocolate pastry cream into the pie shell and leave to set.
Whisk the egg whites and gradually add 150 g/5 oz of the sugar, beating constantly until stiff and firm. Spoon the meringue over the filling, slightly overlapping the pastry, and sprinkle with the remaining sugar. Bake in a preheated oven for 5 minutes or until the meringue begins to colour.
Makes one 23 cm/9 inch pie

Profiteroles au chocolat

Metric
65 g plain flour
1 × 2.5 ml spoon salt
50 g unsalted butter
120 ml water
2 eggs
1 egg beaten with 2 × 15
  ml spoons milk

Imperial
2½ oz plain flour
½ teaspoon salt
2 oz unsalted butter
4 fl oz water
2 eggs
1 egg beaten with 2
  tablespoons milk

Filling:
Chocolate Ice Cream
  (page 64)
Chocolate Butter Sauce
  (page 68), to serve

Filling:
Chocolate Ice Cream
  (page 64)
Chocolate Butter Sauce
  (page 68), to serve

Preparation time: 35 minutes
Cooking time: 25–30 minutes
Oven: 200°C, 400°F, Gas Mark 6

Butter a baking sheet and cover with greaseproof paper. To make the choux dough, sift the flour and salt together on to a sheet of greaseproof paper. Put the butter and water in a saucepan over a low heat, until the butter melts. Increase the heat and bring to the boil. Remove from the heat immediately and add all the flour. Stir the mixture until combined, then place over a medium heat stirring constantly, until the mixture forms a ball that comes away cleanly from the sides of the pan. Remove from the heat and leave to cool for a few minutes.

Add the eggs, 1 at a time, beating after each addition, until thoroughly incorporated. Continue beating until the mixture is smooth.

Spoon the mixture into a piping bag fitted with a 2 cm/¾ inch plain nozzle and pipe 15 walnut-sized pieces of dough, 4 cm/1½ inches apart, on to the baking sheet. Gently brush the top of each choux ball with the egg and milk mixture. Bake in a preheated oven for 15–20 minutes or until the choux balls are golden in colour. A few minutes before they are done, pierce them with a fork to release the steam. Remove from the oven to cool.

When cool, slice each profiterole in half horizontally. Working quickly, spoon the chocolate ice cream on to the bottom half, then replace the top. Place the profiteroles in the freezer for 10 minutes to firm the ice cream, then serve with chocolate butter sauce.
Makes 15

Chiffon pie

Metric
1 quantity Rich
  Shortcrust Pastry (page
  40)

Imperial
1 quantity Rich
  Shortcrust Pastry (page
  40)

Filling:
250 ml milk
120 g sugar
200 g plain chocolate,
  broken into pieces
2 eggs, separated, whites
  stiffly beaten
1 × 15 ml spoon powdered
  gelatine
3 × 15 ml spoons strong
  black coffee
350 ml double cream,
  whipped

Filling:
8 fl oz milk
4½ oz sugar
7 oz plain chocolate,
  broken into pieces
2 eggs, separated, whites
  stiffly beaten
1 tablespoon powdered
  gelatine
3 tablespoons strong
  black coffee
12 fl oz double cream,
  whipped

Topping:
250 ml double or whipping
  cream, whipped
grated chocolate

Topping:
8 fl oz double or whipping
  cream, whipped
grated chocolate

Preparation time: 20 minutes, plus chilling
Cooking time: about 1 hour
Oven: 190°C, 375°F, Gas Mark 5

On a floured work surface, roll the pastry out to a thickness of 3–5 mm/⅛–¼ inch and line a 23 cm/9 inch fluted deep pie tin. Cover with greaseproof paper weighted with beans or rice and bake blind in a preheated oven for 15 minutes until the edges are lightly coloured. Remove the paper and weights and bake for another 15 minutes or until the base is lightly coloured. Remove to a wire tray and leave to cool before removing the tin.

To make the filling, combine the milk, 75 g/3 oz of the sugar and the chocolate pieces in a saucepan and cook over a medium heat. Stir constantly as the chocolate melts, until the mixture thickens and is smooth. Remove from the heat and leave to cool for a few minutes, then whisk in the egg yolks.

Dissolve the gelatine with the coffee over a low heat and stir into the warm chocolate mixture. Chill until the mixture begins to set. Whisk the remaining sugar into the beaten egg whites until firm. Gently fold the cream and then the beaten egg whites into the chocolate mixture. Pour into the pie shell and decorate with whipped cream and grated chocolate.
Makes one 20 cm/8 inch pie

From the front: Chiffon pie; Profiteroles au chocolat

Mousse éclairs

Metric
1 quantity Choux Pastry
  (page 32)
1 egg beaten with 2 × 15
  ml spoons milk
1 quantity Chocolate
  Mousse (page 45)
Chocolate Cream
  Sauce (page 69)
double or whipping cream,
  whipped (optional)

Imperial
1 quantity Choux Pastry
  (page 32)
1 egg beaten with 2
  tablespoons milk
1 quantity Chocolate
  Mousse (page 45)
Chocolate Cream
  Sauce (page 69)
double or whipping cream,
  whipped (optional)

Preparation time: 40 minutes, plus chilling
Cooking time: 25 minutes
Oven: 200°C, 400°F, Gas Mark 6; 190°C, 375°F, Gas
  Mark 5

This recipe incorporates a chocolate mousse, which
needs to be prepared one day in advance.

Butter a baking sheet and cover with greaseproof
paper. To form the eclairs, spoon the choux dough
into a piping bag, fitted with a 1 cm/½ inch plain
nozzle and pipe the dough on to the baking sheet in
10 strips 7.5–10 cm/3–4 inches long, and 4 cm/1½
inches apart. Gently brush the top of each with the
egg and milk mixture.
Bake the eclairs in a preheated oven for 15 minutes,
reduce the heat and bake for 10 minutes more or until
they are golden in colour. A few minutes before they
are done, pierce the ends of each with a knife to
release the steam. Remove from the oven to cool.
When cool, slice each 1 in half lengthwise and spoon
some of the chocolate mousse on to the bottom half.
Replace the tops and chill until ready to serve. Spoon
the chocolate cream sauce over each 1 before serving
and, if using, decorate each with the whipped cream.
Makes 10

Chocolate choux tart

Metric
½ quantity Rich
  Shortcrust Pastry
  (*page 40*)
1 quantity Choux Pastry
  (*page 32*)
1 egg beaten with 2 × 15
  ml spoons milk

Imperial
½ quantity Rich
  Shortcrust Pastry
  (*page 40*)
1 quantity Choux Pastry
  (*page 32*)
1 egg beaten with 2
  tablespoons milk

**Chocolate pastry
cream:**
5 egg yolks
100 g sugar
45 g plain flour, sifted
pinch of salt
475 ml milk
100 g plain chocolate,
  broken into pieces
2 × 5 ml spoons powdered
  gelatine
2 × 15 ml spoons cold
  water
40 g caster sugar
4 egg whites, stiffly
  beaten

**Chocolate pastry
cream:**
5 egg yolks
4 oz sugar
1 ¾ oz plain flour, sifted
pinch of salt
16 fl oz milk
4 oz plain chocolate,
  broken into pieces
2 teaspoons powdered
  gelatine
2 tablespoons cold
  water
1 ½ oz caster sugar
4 egg whites, stiffly
  beaten

To finish:
225 g sugar
lemon juice
chocolate scrolls (*optional*)
icing sugar

To finish:
8 oz sugar
lemon juice
chocolate scrolls (*optional*)
icing sugar

Preparation time: 50 minutes
Cooking time: about 1 hour
Oven: 200°C, 400°F, Gas Mark 6

An interesting variation of the classic Gâteau St Honoré, named after the patron saint of pastry cooks, a 7th century bishop.

Roll out the shortcrust pastry 5 mm/¼ inch thick. Using a plate as a guide, cut the dough into a 20 cm/8 inch circle. Place this on a baking sheet and prick it with a fork. Spoon the choux dough into a piping bag fitted with a 2 cm/¾ inch plain nozzle and pipe an edge of choux round the rim. Glaze the choux with some of the egg and milk mixture.
Butter a baking sheet and line with greaseproof paper. Pipe 15 walnut-sized pieces of dough, 4 cm/1½ inches apart on to the prepared baking sheet, glazing the top of each with the egg and milk. Bake the choux balls in a preheated oven for 15–20 minutes and the base for 25–30 minutes or until golden brown. A few minutes before they are done, prick first the choux balls, then the choux ring with a fork to release the steam. Remove from the oven and cool on a wire tray.
To make the chocolate pastry cream filling, beat the egg yolks and sugar together in a mixing bowl until thick and light. Gradually stir in the flour and salt.
Heat the milk with the chocolate pieces in a heavy saucepan and stir until the chocolate melts and the mixture is smooth. Slowly pour the hot milk into the egg mixture, stirring constantly. Pour the mixture back into the pan, and, stirring constantly over a medium heat, bring the mixture to the boil. Cook the chocolate pastry cream for 2 minutes more, then remove from the heat.
To fill the choux balls, cool a third of the pastry cream in a bowl, then pipe it inside.
To fill the tart, soften the gelatine with the water in a saucepan. Place the pan over a low heat to dissolve the gelatine, then stir it into the remaining warmed pastry cream. Beat the sugar into the egg whites until stiff, then gradually fold in the pastry cream. Reserve for filling the tart.
To finish the tart, place the sugar and a few drops of lemon juice in a heavy saucepan. Cook over a low heat, stirring constantly, until all the sugar is dissolved and the caramel is clear and just turned golden. Remove from the heat and dip the base of the pan in cold water to arrest further cooking. Dip the base of each choux ball into the caramel and place on to the choux pastry ring, then spoon some of the remaining caramel over each one.
Fill the pastry case with the reserved pastry cream and (if using) decorate with chocolate scrolls. Lightly dust the scrolls with icing sugar.
Makes one 20 cm/8 inch tart

Mousse éclairs with Chocolate cream sauce; Chocolate choux tart

Palmiers

Metric	Imperial
450 g unsalted butter	1 lb unsalted butter
450 g plain flour	1 lb plain flour
2 × 5 ml spoons salt	2 teaspoons salt
150–200 ml water	¼–⅓ pint water

To finish:	To finish:
40 g sugar	1 ½ oz sugar
175 g plain chocolate, coarsely grated	6 oz plain chocolate, coarsely grated

Preparation time: 45 minutes, plus chilling
Cooking time: 10–20 minutes
Oven: 220°C, 425°F, Gas Mark 7

Puff pastry is easiest to make using the proportions given. If fewer palmiers are required, divide the pastry once made and store half in the refrigerator or freezer. Halve the other ingredients before using them.

Place 350 g/12 oz of the butter between 2 sheets of greaseproof paper and roll it into a square slab about 1 cm/½ inch thick. Chill for 30 minutes.
Sift the flour and salt into a mixing bowl and add the remaining butter cut into small pieces. Using the fingertips, rub the butter into the flour. Add just enough water to bind the ingredients and shape into a ball. Wrap the dough in lightly floured cling film and chill for 30 minutes.
On a lightly floured board roll the dough into a 30 cm/12 inch square. Place the square of butter diagonally in the centre of the dough and fold each corner of the dough over the butter, so that they meet in the centre like an envelope. Gently roll the dough into a rectangle, 3 times as long as it is wide.
Fold the dough in thirds, to make 3 layers. Give the dough a quarter turn, so that the folded edges are at the side and roll into a rectangle. Fold into thirds again, wrap in cling film and chill for 30 minutes. Repeat twice more, giving the dough 6 turns in all. Wrap and chill for 1 hour before using.
Lightly butter a baking sheet. On a lightly floured board, divide the dough in half and roll into 2 rectangles 15 × 38 cm/6 × 15 inches, and 3 mm/⅛ inch thick. Sprinkle generously with sugar, then cover with the chopped chocolate. Fold each short side into the centre and then fold again in half. Using a knife dipped in flour, cut the dough into slices about 1 cm/½ inch thick. Place on the baking sheet and bake in a preheated oven for 10–15 minutes or until golden brown.
Makes about 50

Crackling pie

Metric	Imperial
175 g ground almonds	6 oz ground almonds
50 g caster sugar	2 oz caster sugar
1 × 5 ml spoon rum	1 teaspoon rum
1 egg white, beaten	1 egg white, beaten

Filling:	Filling:
250 ml double cream	8 fl oz double cream
225 g plain chocolate, broken into pieces	8 oz plain chocolate, broken into pieces
1 egg yolk	1 egg yolk
1 × 15 ml spoon icing sugar	1 tablespoon icing sugar
1 × 15 ml spoon rum	1 tablespoon rum

Topping:	Topping:
4 egg whites, stiffly beaten	4 egg whites, stiffly beaten
100 g caster sugar	4 oz caster sugar
25 g flaked almonds	1 oz flaked almonds

Preparation time: 30 minutes, plus cooling
Cooking time: 40–50 minutes
Oven: 180°C, 350°F, Gas Mark 4;
    230°C, 450°F, Gas Mark 8

Butter a 20 cm/8 inch flan tin. Combine the almonds, sugar, rum and beaten egg white, and work to a stiff paste. Shape into a ball, wrap in cling film and chill for 30 minutes. Flour a work surface and roll out the paste to line the tin. If the paste breaks, gently press it into the tin. Line the inside edge of the shell with a strip of foil and bake in a preheated oven for 20–25 minutes or until lightly browned. Remove to a wire tray and leave until cool before carefully removing the foil and tin.
To prepare the filling, place the cream and chocolate pieces in a saucepan over a low heat. Stir constantly until the chocolate melts and the mixture is thick and smooth. Remove from the heat and leave to cool slightly. Stir in the egg yolk. Add the icing sugar and rum and beat until light and fluffy. Fill the almond shell with the chocolate mixture.
For the topping, gradually add the sugar to the beaten egg whites, until firm and glossy. Spread the meringue over the chocolate, slightly overlapping the shell. Scatter the flaked almonds over the top and bake in a preheated oven at the higher temperature for 5 minutes or until the meringue is lightly browned.
Makes one 20 cm/8 inch flan

Clockwise from top: Palmiers;
Crackling pie; Chocolate chip tartlets

Chocolate chip tartlets

Preparation time: 25 minutes
Cooking time: 25–30 minutes
Oven: 180°C, 350°F, Gas Mark 4

Metric
1 quantity Rich
  Shortcrust Pastry (page
  40)

Filling:
75 g unsalted butter
65 g sugar
25 g vanilla sugar
2 eggs
1 × 5 ml spoon rum
  (optional)
1½ × 5 ml spoons plain
  flour
40 g chopped walnuts
175 g plain chocolate,
  roughly chopped

Imperial
1 quantity Rich
  Shortcrust Pastry (page
  40)

Filling:
3 oz unsalted butter
2½ oz sugar
1 oz vanilla sugar
2 eggs
1 teaspoon rum
  (optional)
1½ teaspoons plain
  flour
1½ oz chopped walnuts
6 oz plain chocolate,
  roughly chopped

On a floured work surface, roll the pastry out to a thickness of 3 mm/⅛ inch. With a 7.5 cm/3 inch pastry cutter, cut into 18 circles. Gently press the dough into 18 tartlet tins and prick the shells thoroughly with a fork. Place on a baking sheet and chill while making the filling.

Beat the butter in a mixing bowl, until pale and soft. Add the sugars and beat until light and fluffy. Beat in the eggs, 1 at a time, beating well after each addition. Stir in the rum (if using), flour, walnuts and chocolate.

Fill each tartlet shell with a heaped 5 ml spoon/teaspoon of the mixture and bake in a preheated oven for 25–30 minutes or until lightly golden on top. Remove to a wire tray and leave to cool. The tartlets can be served either warm or cold.

Makes 18

Chocolate cream tartlets

Metric
1 quantity Rich
  Shortcrust Pastry (page
  40)
175 g plain chocolate,
  broken into pieces
50 ml strong black coffee
1 × 15 ml spoon brandy
2 egg yolks
300 ml double cream,
  whipped

Topping:
150 ml double or whipping
  cream
2 × 5 ml spoons vanilla
  sugar
grated chocolate

Imperial
1 quantity Rich
  Shortcrust Pastry (page
  40)
6 oz plain chocolate,
  broken into pieces
2 fl oz strong black coffee
1 tablespoon brandy
2 egg yolks
½ pint double cream,
  whipped

Topping:
¼ pint double or whipping
  cream
2 teaspoons vanilla
  sugar
grated chocolate

Preparation time: 30 minutes
Cooking time: 30 minutes
Oven: 190°C, 375°F, Gas Mark 5

If larger tartlets are preferred, cut the pastry into 10 cm/4 inch circles and use to line 6 tartlet tins.

On a floured work surface, roll the pastry out to a thickness of 3 mm/⅛ inch and, with a 7.5 cm/3 inch pastry cutter, cut into 12 circles. Gently press the dough into 12 tartlet tins and prick the shells thoroughly with a fork. Place on a baking sheet and bake in a preheated oven for 15 minutes or until golden brown. Remove from the oven and cool on a wire tray, before removing the tins.

To make the filling, melt the chocolate with the coffee and brandy in a saucepan over a low heat, stirring constantly as the chocolate melts and forms a thick paste. Cool slightly and stir in the egg yolks. Continue stirring until cool. Gently fold in the cream and divide the mixture between the tartlets. Chill until set.

In a chilled bowl, whisk the cream with the vanilla sugar until it is thick and forms soft peaks. Decorate each tartlet with a spoonful of this topping and some grated chocolate. Serve cold.

Makes 12

Chocolate strudel

Metric
100 g plain flour
65 ml water
½ beaten egg
½ × 5 ml spoon salt
75 g unsalted butter,
    melted and cooled
dash of vinegar

Imperial
4 oz plain flour
2 ½ fl oz water
½ beaten egg
½ teaspoon salt
3 oz unsalted butter,
    melted and cooled
dash of vinegar

Filling:
40 g unsalted butter
50 g vanilla sugar
2 eggs, separated, whites
    stiffly beaten
50 g plain chocolate,
    grated
65 g chopped walnuts
40 g seedless raisins
65 ml double cream
pinch ground
    cinnamon
1 ½ × 15 ml spoons caster
    sugar
icing sugar

Filling:
1 ½ oz unsalted butter
2 oz vanilla sugar
2 eggs, separated, whites
    stiffly beaten
2 oz plain chocolate,
    grated
2 ½ oz chopped walnuts
1 ½ oz seedless raisins
2 ½ fl oz double cream
pinch ground
    cinnamon
1 ½ tablespoons caster
    sugar
icing sugar

Preparation time: 1¼ hours
Cooking time: 40 minutes
Oven: 190°C, 375°F, Gas Mark 5

Sift the flour into a mixing bowl and make a well in the centre. Lightly beat together the water, egg, salt, 1 × 15 ml spoon/1 tablespoon of the butter and the vinegar, and pour the mixture into the well. Incorporate all the ingredients by hand. Beat the dough against a well floured surface until the dough is smooth and elastic. Knead on a floured work surface for 10–15 minutes. Place in a well floured bowl covered with a cloth and leave to rest for 30 minutes. To make the filling, beat the butter in a mixing bowl, until pale and smooth. Add the vanilla sugar and beat until light and fluffy. Add the egg yolks, 1 at a time, beating well after each addition. Add the chocolate, walnuts, raisins, cream and cinnamon, and mix well. In another bowl, whisk the caster sugar with the egg whites until stiff. Gently fold a third of the egg whites into the chocolate mixture and then fold in the remainder.

Cover a table top with a large clean cloth, dusted with flour. Place the dough in the centre of the cloth and brush the top with some of the remaining melted butter.

Working in all directions, roll the dough out 3 mm/⅛ inch thick. Brush it with more of the butter and, working with floured hands, slip your hands beneath the dough and stretch it from the centre, working outwards. Carefully stretch it as thin as possible, working all around the table to avoid tearing the dough. Trim the dough into a rectangle about 36 cm/14 inches wide and 46 cm/18 inches long.

Butter a large baking sheet. Spoon the filling along one short side of the pastry leaving a 5 cm/2 inch margin on the bottom and sides. Fold the 3 narrow margins over the filling, so that it is well wrapped. Brush the remaining pastry with melted butter, then gently lift the cloth, so that the dough gradually rolls itself up. Roll the dough on to the baking sheet and bake in a preheated oven, basting occasionally with the rest of the melted butter, for 40 minutes or until crisp and golden. Remove the strudel from the oven and dust with icing sugar. The strudel is best served warm, but may be eaten cold.
Makes one 36 cm/14 inch strudel

Chocolate cream tartlets; Chocolate strudel

Tarte au chocolat

Metric
225 g plain flour
2 × 15 ml spoons caster
   sugar
1 × 5 ml spoon salt
50 g ground almonds
   (optional)
150 g unsalted butter, cut
   into pieces
1 egg yolk

Filling:
200 ml double cream
1 ½ × 15 ml spoons brandy
200 g plain chocolate,
   broken into pieces
2 egg whites, stiffly beaten
50 g caster sugar

Topping:
300 ml double or whipping
   cream
1 ½ × 15 ml spoons vanilla
   sugar
crushed Praline (page 44),
   to decorate

Imperial
8 oz plain flour
2 tablespoons caster
   sugar
1 teaspoon salt
2 oz ground almonds
   (optional)
5 oz unsalted butter, cut
   into pieces
1 egg yolk

Filling:
⅓ pint double cream
1 ½ tablespoons brandy
7 oz plain chocolate,
   broken into pieces
2 egg whites, stiffly beaten
2 oz caster sugar

Topping:
½ pint double or whipping
   cream
1 ½ tablespoons vanilla
   sugar
crushed Praline (page 44),
   to decorate

Preparation time: 25 minutes, plus chilling
Cooking time: about 45 minutes
Oven: 190°C, 375°F, Gas Mark 5

To make the pastry, sift the flour, sugar, salt and almonds (if using) into a mound on a work surface, or in a mixing bowl. Make a well in the centre of the mound and add the butter and egg yolk. Using the fingertips, work quickly to incorporate all the ingredients. Shape the dough into a ball, wrap it in cling film or foil and chill for 1 hour.

On a floured work surface, roll the dough out to a thickness of 3–5 mm/⅛–¼ inch and line a 25 cm/10 inch flan tin. Cover with greaseproof paper, weighted with beans or rice and bake blind in a preheated oven for 15 minutes until the edges are lightly coloured. Remove the paper and weights and bake for another 15 minutes or until the base is lightly coloured. Remove to a wire tray and leave to cool in the tin.

To prepare the filling, pour the cream and brandy into a saucepan and bring just to the boil. Add the chocolate pieces and stir until the chocolate melts and the mixture is thick and smooth. Leave to chill for at least 1 hour before whisking until light and fluffy.

Beat the egg whites with the sugar until stiff. Gently fold a third of this mixture into the chocolate and then fold in the rest. Remove the pastry case from the tin and fill evenly with the chocolate mixture.

Whisk the cream with the vanilla sugar in a mixing bowl, until light and fluffy, holding soft peaks. Spread the cream over the top of the pie and decorate with the crushed praline.

Makes one 25 cm/10 inch flan

Churros con chocolate

Metric
2 quantities Choux
   Pastry (page 32)
1 × 15 ml spoon rum
oil, for deep frying
caster sugar
Spiced Chocolate Cup
   (page 67) or French
   Chocolate (page 67), to
   serve

Imperial
2 quantities Choux Pastry
   (page 32)
1 tablespoon rum
oil, for deep frying
caster sugar
Spiced Chocolate Cup
   (page 67) or French
   Chocolate (page 67), to
   serve

Preparation time: 20 minutes
Cooking time: 5–7 minutes per batch

Flavour the prepared choux pastry with the rum and spoon into a piping bag fitted with a plain or star nozzle. Heat the oil in a deep, heavy bottomed pan to 180°– 190°C/350°–375°F, or until a cube of bread browns in 30 seconds. Pipe 5–7.5 cm/2–3 inch lengths of dough into the oil and fry for 5–7 minutes or until golden brown. Remove the pastries with a slotted spoon on to absorbent paper towels to drain. Repeat with the remaining dough.

Sprinkle the churros with sugar and serve warm or cold with spiced chocolate cup or French chocolate.

Tarte au chocolat; Churros con chocolate

HOT AND COLD DESSERTS

The ideas here include rich, full-flavoured desserts, such as the marquise and the steamed pudding, served with custard sauce or cream, as well as lighter recipes, where the chocolate flavour is an accompaniment to fruit or meringue, as in poached pears or oeufs à la neige. Some of the desserts cooked in moulds are set in a bain marie. This can be any ovenproof dish, pan or casserole, large enough to take both the mould and the water surrounding it. The effect is to disperse the heat evenly through the mixture without drying it out.

Poached pears with chocolate

Metric
4 firm, slightly under-ripe
  eating pears, peeled,
  halved and cored
600 ml good red wine
65 g sugar

Imperial
4 firm, slightly under-ripe
  eating pears, peeled,
  halved and cored
1 pint good red wine
2½ oz sugar

To decorate:
175–225 g chocolate
  scrolls
icing sugar

To decorate:
6–8 oz chocolate
  scrolls
icing sugar

Preparation time: 5 minutes
Cooking time: about 1¼ hours

Place the pears in a heavy saucepan and cover with the wine and sugar. Bring to the boil, reduce the heat, cover and simmer for about 1 hour or until tender. Remove with a slotted spoon and keep warm.
Reduce the liquid over a high heat, until it has the consistency of a syrup. Decorate 4 dessert plates with a layer of chocolate scrolls and lightly dust with icing sugar. Place 2 pear halves on top of the chocolate on each plate and spoon some of the syrup over them. Serve immediately.

Almond and chocolate soufflé; Poached pears with chocolate

Almond and chocolate soufflé

Metric
25 g Praline Powder (page
  44)
120 ml milk
25 g vanilla sugar
50 g lightly roasted
  almonds, finely chopped
50 g plain chocolate,
  broken into pieces
1 × 15 ml spoon plain
  flour, mixed with 2–4
  × 15 ml spoons cold
  milk, to form a slurry
10 g unsalted butter
3 egg yolks
4 egg whites, stiffly beaten

Imperial
1 oz Praline Powder (page
  44)
4 fl oz milk
1 oz vanilla sugar
2 oz lightly roasted
  almonds, finely chopped
2 oz plain chocolate,
  broken into pieces
1 tablespoon plain flour,
  mixed with 2–4
  tablespoons cold milk,
  to form a slurry
¼ oz unsalted butter
3 egg yolks
4 egg whites, stiffly beaten

Preparation time: 30 minutes
Cooking time: 30–40 minutes
Oven: 180°C, 350°F, Gas Mark 4

Butter a 900 ml–1 litre/1½–1¾ pint soufflé dish and sprinkle with the praline powder. Bring the milk, vanilla sugar and almonds just to the boil in a small saucepan. Add the chocolate pieces and the flour to the milk mixture; stir until the chocolate melts and the mixture is smooth. Remove from the heat and leave to cool for a few minutes, then whisk in the butter and egg yolks. Gently fold a quarter of the egg whites into the chocolate mixture and pour this over the remaining egg whites. Gently fold the egg whites into the chocolate.
Pour the mixture into the dish, smooth the top and bake in a preheated oven for 20–25 minutes or until the soufflé is well risen. Serve immediately.

Praline

Metric
175 g nuts (see below)
225 g sugar
65 ml water

Imperial
6 oz nuts (see below)
8 oz sugar
2 ½ fl oz water

Preparation time: 5–10 minutes
Cooking time: 15 minutes
Oven: 180°C, 350°F, Gas Mark 4

Praline, usually made with almonds, can be made with any hard nut such as hazelnuts, walnuts or pistachio nuts. Use whole or chopped nuts, skinned or unskinned, toasted or plain, but if making praline powder the nuts should be peeled.

Place the nuts on a baking sheet and warm them in a preheated oven for 5 minutes. Butter a marble slab or a 25 cm/10 inch square tin.
Place the sugar and water in a heavy saucepan over a medium heat and stir until the sugar dissolves. Brush off any sugar crystals that have formed on the sides of the pan, with a pastry brush dipped in cold water. Bring to the boil and cook until a light caramel colour. Remove the pan from the heat and dip its base in cold water to arrest further cooking. Stir in the warmed nuts and pour immediately on the marble slab or into the tin. When the praline is completely cold, break it into pieces.

Variation:
For crushed praline, put praline pieces into a plastic bag and crush with a rolling pin into small pieces. For praline powder, put the pieces into a plastic bag and crush into fine powder, or pulverize in a coffee grinder.
Makes 350 g/12 oz

Rich chocolate mousse

Metric	Imperial
200 g plain chocolate, broken into pieces	7 oz plain chocolate, broken into pieces
3 × 15 ml spoons water	3 tablespoons water
25 g unsalted butter, cut cut into pieces	1 oz unsalted butter, cut into pieces
4 eggs, separated, whites stiffly beaten	4 eggs, separated, whites stiffly beaten
1 × 15 ml spoon rum or brandy (optional)	1 tablespoon rum or brandy (optional)
175 ml double or whipping cream, whipped	6 fl oz double or whipping cream, whipped
crushed Praline (page 44)	crushed Praline (page 44)

Preparation time: 15 minutes, plus setting
Cooking time: about 15 minutes

Stir the chocolate pieces with the water in a saucepan over a low heat. Continue stirring until the chocolate melts and forms a smooth paste. Remove from the heat. Stir in the butter, then the egg yolks, 1 at a time, and continue stirring until the mixture is smooth and glossy. Add the brandy or rum, if using, and mix well.
Add a spoonful of the chocolate mixture to the beaten egg whites and whisk very gently to blend the ingredients. Gently fold the egg whites mixture into the remaining chocolate. Pour the mousse into a 900 ml/1½ pint bowl or spoon it into 4 serving glasses. Leave to chill at least 2 hours and decorate with the whipped cream, sprinkled with praline.

Chocolate marquise;
Rich chocolate mousse sprinkled with crushed Praline

Chocolate marquise

Metric	Imperial
14 sponge finger biscuits	14 sponge finger biscuits
½ × 15 ml spoon strong black coffee	½ tablespoon strong black coffee
3 egg yolks	3 egg yolks
150 g caster sugar	5 oz caster sugar
65 g plain chocolate, melted and cooled slightly	2½ oz plain chocolate, melted and cooled slightly
1 × 15 ml spoon brandy	1 tablespoon brandy
165 g unsalted butter, softened	5½ oz unsalted butter, softened
65 g cocoa powder	2½ oz cocoa powder
275 ml double cream, whipped	9 fl oz double cream, whipped
Custard Sauce (page 67), to serve	Custard Sauce (page 67), to serve

Preparation time: 40 minutes, plus chilling

This is an extremely rich, yet surprisingly light dessert.

Line the bottom of a 450 g/1 lb loaf tin with grease-proof paper. Brush the biscuits with the coffee and trim them to line the loaf tin. Reserve the crumbs.
Whisk the egg yolks with the sugar in a mixing bowl, until the mixture falls off the whisk in a thick ribbon. Gently fold in the chocolate and the brandy.
In another mixing bowl, beat the butter until it is pale and creamy. Gradually add the cocoa powder and beat until the mixture is thoroughly blended.
Add the cocoa mixture to the chocolate mixture and mix together thoroughly. Whisk in the whipped cream and the reserved biscuit crumbs until all the ingredients are blended. Spread the chocolate cream into the tin and chill for 3 hours or until set. Unmould and cut in slices. Serve with custard sauce.
Serves 4–6

Chocolate blinis

Preparation time: 25–30 minutes, plus rising
Cooking time: 10–15 minutes

Metric
25 ml warm water
10 g dried yeast
40 g buckwheat or
   wholewheat flour
50 g plain flour
25 g cocoa powder
150 ml warm milk
2 eggs, separated, whites
   stiffly beaten
1 × 1.25 ml spoon salt
50 g caster sugar
25 g unsalted butter,
   melted
200 ml soured cream

Imperial
1 fl oz warm water
¼ oz dried yeast
1½ oz buckwheat or
   wholewheat flour
2 oz plain flour
1 oz cocoa powder
¼ pint warm milk
2 eggs, separated, whites
   stiffly beaten
¼ teaspoon salt
2 oz caster sugar
1 oz unsalted butter,
   melted
⅓ pint soured cream

Mix the warm water and yeast and leave for 15 minutes. Sift 15 g/½ oz of the buckwheat or wholewheat flour, all of the plain flour and cocoa powder together into a mixing bowl. Make a well in the centre and add the yeast and 100 ml/3½ fl oz of the warm milk. Stir to combine the ingredients and beat until smooth and creamy. Cover with a towel and leave to rise for about 1 hour or until doubled in bulk.

When risen, beat down by hand and stir in the remaining buckwheat or wholewheat flour. Cover with the towel and leave in a warm place for 2 hours. Stir the batter, add the remaining milk, egg yolks, salt, sugar, melted butter and 2½ × 15 ml spoons/ 2½ tablespoons of the soured cream. Stir until thoroughly blended. Gently fold in a third of the beaten egg whites, then fold in the rest. Cover with the towel and leave for 30 minutes.

Heat the butter in a heavy frying pan over a medium heat. Place spoonfuls of batter in the frying pan, leaving enough room between each pancake to turn them. Cook the pancakes about 2 minutes on each side or until lightly coloured.

Serve hot with the remaining soured cream.
Serves 6–8

Crêpes soufflés

Metric	Imperial
100 g plain flour	4 oz plain flour
pinch of salt	pinch of salt
25 g caster sugar	1 oz caster sugar
2 eggs	2 eggs
about 300 ml milk	about ½ pint milk
25 g unsalted butter, melted	1 oz unsalted butter, melted
oil	oil

Filling:

Almond and Chocolate Soufflé mixture (page 43)	Almond and Chocolate Soufflé mixture (page 43)
caster sugar	caster sugar
Custard Sauce (page 67) or whipped cream, to serve	Custard Sauce (page 67) or whipped cream, to serve

Preparation time: 55 minutes
Cooking time: 15–20 minutes
Oven: 200°C, 400°F, Gas Mark 6

An elegant and exciting showpiece for everyone to enjoy at table. It is simple and quick to prepare if the crepes are made in advance.

Sift the flour, salt and sugar into a mixing bowl and add the eggs. Whisk in the milk and beat only until smooth, then stir in the melted butter. The batter should have the consistency of single cream; add more milk if necessary.

To make the crêpes, heat a 15 cm/6 inch pancake or omelette pan over a medium heat with a small amount of oil. Ladle in enough batter just to cover the bottom of the pan and rotate to coat the bottom as thinly as possible. Pour out any excess batter and trim away the trail. After about 10 seconds, when the surface of the crêpe appears dry and the edges free themselves from the sides, turn the crêpe over. Cook for a few seconds and slide the crêpe on to a plate. Repeat until all the batter is used. If the surface of the pan looks dry, wipe with a greased paper.

Butter a large ovenproof dish. Place a generous spoonful of the soufflé mixture on to one half of each crêpe. Fold over the other half and place on the dish. Rest a piece of kitchen foil lightly over the top of each crêpe to prevent it from burning and bake in a preheated oven for 8 minutes.

Serve the crêpes with custard sauce or cream.

Serves 6

Clockwise from top: Crêpes à la crème; Chocolate blinis; Crêpes soufflés

Crêpes à la crème

Metric	Imperial
225 g plain flour	8 oz plain flour
1 × 1.25 ml spoon salt	¼ teaspoon salt
50 g caster sugar	2 oz caster sugar
4 eggs	4 eggs
about 600 ml milk	about 1 pint milk
50 g unsalted butter, melted	2 oz unsalted butter, melted
2 × 15 ml spoons brandy	2 tablespoons brandy
oil	oil

Filling:

4 egg yolks	4 egg yolks
65 g sugar	2 ½ oz sugar
40 g vanilla sugar	1 ½ oz vanilla sugar
300 ml double cream	½ pint double cream
breadcrumbs	breadcrumbs
200 g walnuts, finely chopped	7 oz walnuts, finely chopped
225 g grated chocolate	8 oz grated chocolate
Custard Sauce (page 67) or whipped cream, to serve	Custard Sauce (page 67) or whipped cream, to serve

Preparation time: 55 minutes
Cooking time: 40 minutes
Oven: 160°C, 325°F, Gas Mark 3

Sift the flour, salt and sugar into a mixing bowl and add the eggs. Whisk in the milk and beat only until smooth, then stir in the melted butter and brandy. The batter should have the consistency of single cream; add more milk if necessary.

To make the crêpes, heat a 15 cm/6 inch pancake or omelette pan over a medium heat with a small amount of oil. Ladle in enough batter just to cover the bottom of the pan and rotate to coat the bottom as thinly as possible. Pour out any excess batter and trim away the trail. After about 10 seconds, when the surface of the crêpe appears dry and the edges free themselves from the sides, turn the crêpe over. Cook for a few seconds and slide the crêpe on to a plate. Repeat until all the batter is used. If the surface of the pan looks dry, wipe with greased paper.

To make the filling, beat the egg yolks and sugars until pale and creamy. Beat in the cream and mix well. Butter an 18 cm/7 inch cake tin and sprinkle it with the breadcrumbs. Place the crepes in the mould in layers, spooning some of the filling and sprinkling some of the walnuts and chocolate over each layer. Finish with a crêpe and cover with a round of buttered greaseproof paper. Bake in a pre-heated oven for 30 minutes or until the custard has set. Remove and leave to cool for 15–20 minutes. Turn out and serve warm with custard sauce or whipped cream.

Serves 6–8

Individual chocolate soufflés

Preparation time: 20 minutes
Cooking time: 20–25 minutes
Oven: 200°C, 400°F, Gas Mark 6

Metric
caster sugar, for sprinkling
120 ml milk
25 g vanilla sugar
1 × 15 ml spoon Grand
  Marnier or brandy
65 g plain chocolate,
  broken into pieces
1 × 15 ml spoon plain
  flour, mixed with 2–4
  × 15 ml spoons cold
  milk, to form a slurry
10 g unsalted butter
3 egg yolks
4 egg whites, stiffly beaten
3 × 15 ml spoons plain
  chopped chocolate

Imperial
caster sugar, for sprinkling
4 fl oz milk
1 oz vanilla sugar
1 tablespoon Grand
  Marnier or brandy
2½ oz plain chocolate,
  broken into pieces
1 tablespoon plain flour,
  mixed with 2–4
  tablespoons cold milk, to
  form a slurry
¼ oz unsalted butter
3 egg yolks
4 egg whites, stiffly beaten
3 tablespoons plain
  chopped chocolate

Butter 6 ramekins and sprinkle with caster sugar. Bring the milk, vanilla sugar and Grand Marnier or brandy just to the boil in a small saucepan. Add the chocolate pieces and the flour and milk mixture. Stir until the chocolate melts and the mixture is smooth. Remove from the heat and leave to cool for a few minutes, then whisk in the butter and egg yolks. Gently fold a quarter of the egg whites into the chocolate mixture and pour this over the remaining egg whites. Gently fold the remaining egg whites into the chocolate.

Divide half of the soufflé mixture between the 6 ramekins and sprinkle 1½ × 5 ml spoons/1½ teaspoons of the chopped chocolate on top of each one. Spoon the remaining mixture over the chocolate and place on a baking sheet. Bake in a preheated oven for 12–15 minutes or until well risen. Serve immediately.
Makes 6

Individual chocolate soufflés; Chocolate waffles;
Steamed chocolate pudding with Custard sauce

Chocolate waffles

Metric	Imperial
50 g plain chocolate, broken into pieces	2 oz plain chocolate, broken into pieces
50 ml water	2 fl oz water
75 g unsalted butter	3 oz unsalted butter
2 eggs	2 eggs
75–90 g sugar	3–3 ½ oz sugar
175 g plain flour	6 oz plain flour
2 × 5 ml spoons baking powder	2 teaspoons baking powder
120 ml milk	4 fl oz milk
75 g chopped walnuts	3 oz chopped walnuts
oil	oil
Chocolate Ice Cream (page 64) or whipped cream, to serve	Chocolate Ice Cream (page 64) or whipped cream, to serve

Preparation time: 10 minutes
Cooking time: about 15 minutes

Stir the chocolate pieces and water together in a saucepan over a low heat, until the chocolate melts and the mixture forms a paste. Off the heat, beat in the butter, then the eggs and finally the sugar. Sift the flour and baking powder together on to a sheet of greaseproof paper and add alternately with the milk. Stir in the walnuts.
Pour the batter into a hot oiled waffle iron. Bring the cover down and cook for 2–3 minutes either side.
Serve the waffles hot with chocolate ice cream or whipped cream.
Serves 6–8

Steamed chocolate pudding

Metric	Imperial
90 g plain chocolate, broken into pieces	3 ½ oz plain chocolate, broken into pieces
65 ml strong black coffee	2 ½ fl oz strong black coffee
75 g unsalted butter, softened	3 oz unsalted butter, softened
3 eggs, separated, whites stiffly beaten	3 eggs, separated, whites stiffly beaten
75 g sugar	3 oz sugar
25 g vanilla sugar	1 oz vanilla sugar
65 g plain flour	2 ½ oz plain flour
Custard Sauce (page 67), to serve	Custard Sauce (page 67), to serve

Preparation time: 15 minutes
Cooking time: about 50 minutes
Oven: 180°C, 350°F, Gas Mark 4

Lavishly butter a Kugelhopf mould. Stir the chocolate pieces and coffee together in a metal mixing bowl over a low heat, until the chocolate melts and forms a paste. Off the heat, beat in the butter, then the egg yolks, sugars and finally the flour. If the mixture stiffens, place over another bowl filled with warm water and stir until a smooth paste is formed.
Gently fold a third of the beaten egg whites into the chocolate mixture, then fold in the rest. Pour the mixture into the mould and place in a bain marie (a tin or casserole filled with hot water to the level of the pudding's surface). Cook in a preheated oven for 40 minutes or until the pudding is firm to the touch. Remove and leave to cool on a wire tray for 15–20 minutes before turning out on a warm serving dish. Serve with custard sauce.

Chocolate liqueur mousse

Metric	Imperial
175–225 g dipping or plain chocolate	6–8 oz dipping or plain chocolate

Mousse:

Metric	Imperial
200 g plain chocolate, broken into pieces	7 oz plain chocolate, broken into pieces
3 × 15 ml spoons water	3 tablespoons water
1 × 2.5 ml spoon finely grated orange rind	½ teaspoon finely grated orange rind
25 g unsalted butter	1 oz unsalted butter
4 egg yolks	4 egg yolks
2 × 15 ml spoons Grand Marnier, Cointreau or Crème de Menthe	2 tablespoons Grand Marnier, Cointreau or Crème de Menthe
4 egg whites, stiffly beaten	4 egg whites, stiffly beaten
175 ml double or whipping cream	6 fl oz double or whipping cream
1 × 15 ml spoon vanilla sugar	1 tablespoon vanilla sugar

Preparation time: 1 hour
Cooking time: about 15 minutes

Line a tray with greaseproof paper. Melt the dipping or plain chocolate. Spread enough chocolate into each of 6 aluminium foil cases (7.5 cm/3 inches in diameter and 5–6 cm/2–2½ inches deep e.g. jam tart cases) to coat the inside evenly. Invert each case once coated on to the greaseproof paper and leave until the chocolate is firm, about 20 minutes.

When firm, spread a second layer of melted chocolate over the first. Invert the cases on to the greaseproof paper. Leave until the chocolate is set hard. When set, gently run your thumbnail between the chocolate and the case and prize away the chocolate shell. Set aside in a cool place.

To make the mousse, stir the chocolate pieces with the water and orange rind in a saucepan over a low heat. Continue stirring until the chocolate melts and forms a smooth paste. Remove from the heat, stir in the butter, then the egg yolks, 1 at a time, and continue stirring until the mixture is smooth and glossy. Stir in the Grand Marnier, Cointreau or Crème de Menthe and mix well.

Add a spoonful of the chocolate mixture to the beaten egg whites, whisking gently to blend the ingredients. Gently fold the egg white mixture into the chocolate. Spoon the mousse into the chocolate cases and chill for at least 2 hours. Just before serving, whisk the cream with the vanilla sugar until it forms soft peaks. Decorate each mousse with a spoonful of the whipped cream.
Serves 6

Chocolate meringue basket; Chocolate liqueur mousse

Chocolate meringue basket

Metric	Imperial
butter, for greasing	butter, for greasing
175 g caster sugar	6 oz caster sugar
3 egg whites, stiffly beaten	3 egg whites, stiffly beaten
1½ × 5 ml spoons cocoa powder	1½ teaspoons cocoa powder

Filling:

Metric	Imperial
165 g plain chocolate, broken into pieces	5½ oz plain cocolate, broken into pieces
2 × 15 ml spoons strong black coffee	2 tablespoons strong black coffee
2 × 15 ml spoons brandy	2 tablespoons brandy
3 egg yolks	3 egg yolks

Topping:

Metric	Imperial
250 ml double or whipping cream	8 fl oz double or whipping cream
2 × 5 ml spoons vanilla sugar	2 teaspoons vanilla sugar
chocolate scrolls, to decorate	chocolate scrolls, to decorate

Preparation time: 30 minutes
Cooking time: 3¼ hours
Oven: 110°C, 225°F, Gas Mark ¼

Line a baking sheet with greaseproof paper, securing each corner with a dot of butter and, using a plate as a guide, pencil a 20 cm/8 inch circle on the paper. Add the sugar to the beaten egg whites, a little at a time, beating well after each addition. Gently fold in the cocoa powder.

Spoon the meringue into a piping bag fitted with a 1 cm/½ inch nozzle and pipe a spiral on to the baking sheet to fill the circle. Pipe 2 extra rings around the outside to form a raised edge. Bake in a preheated oven for 3 hours or until dry and crisp. Remove from the oven and leave the meringue to cool on the tray. Carefully peel away the paper.

To make the filling, stir the chocolate pieces, coffee and brandy in a heatproof mixing bowl over a pan of gently simmering water. Continue stirring as the chocolate melts until the mixture forms a smooth paste. Add the egg yolks, 1 at a time, beating well after each addition. Continue beating until the mixture thickens slightly. Remove from the heat and stir until cool.

Just before serving, spread the chocolate mixture into the meringue case. Whisk the cream with the vanilla sugar, until it forms soft peaks and spread it over the top. Decorate with the chocolate scrolls.
Makes one 20 cm/8 inch basket

Striped Bavarian cream

Metric	Imperial
150 ml milk	¼ pint milk
½ vanilla pod or 1.25 ml spoon vanilla essence	½ vanilla pod or ¼ teaspoon vanilla essence
2 egg yolks	2 egg yolks
50 g caster sugar	2 oz caster sugar
2½ × 5 ml spoons powdered gelatine, dissolved in 2 × 15 ml spoons cold water	2½ teaspoons powdered gelatine, dissolved in 2 tablespoons cold water
150 ml double or whipping cream, whipped	¼ pint double or whipping cream, whipped

Chocolate Cream:	Chocolate Cream:
300 ml milk	½ pint milk
65 g plain chocolate, broken into pieces	2½ oz plain chocolate, broken into pieces
4 egg yolks	4 egg yolks
100 g caster sugar	4 oz caster sugar
1½ × 15 ml spoons powdered gelatine, dissolved in 2 × 15 ml spoons strong black coffee	1½ tablespoons powdered gelatine, dissolved in 2 tablespoons strong black coffee
300 ml double or whipping cream, lightly whipped	½ pint double or whipping cream, lightly whipped
oil, for greasing (optional)	oil, for greasing (optional)
sliced banana, to decorate	sliced banana, to decorate
lemon juice	lemon juice

Preparation time: 35 minutes, plus infusing and chilling
Cooking time: 20–25 minutes

To make the vanilla cream, bring the milk just to the boil in a saucepan and add the vanilla pod or essence. Remove from the heat, cover and leave to infuse for 15 minutes. Whisk the egg yolks with the sugar in a mixing bowl, until the mixture falls off the whisk in a thick ribbon. Slowly add the infused milk, stirring constantly. Stir in the dissolved gelatine. Pour back into the pan, stirring constantly over a low heat, until the mixture thickens and coats the back of a spoon. Strain the mixture into a bowl and cool. When it begins to set, fold in the whipped cream.
To make the chocolate cream, stir the milk with the chocolate pieces over a low heat, until the chocolate melts and the mixture is smooth. Whisk the egg yolks with the sugar and proceed as for the vanilla cream.
Lightly brush a 1.5 litre/2½ pint decorative mould with oil or rinse with cold water. Fill the mould with alternate layers of chocolate and vanilla cream. Pour each layer carefully so that they remain separate. Cover the mould and chill for about 5 hours or until well set. Unmould on to a chilled serving dish. Decorate with banana, sprinkled with lemon juice.
Serves 8

Coffee-chocolate mousse

Metric	Imperial
75 g caster sugar	3 oz caster sugar
3 egg whites, stiffly beaten	3 egg whites, stiffly beaten
oil, for greasing	oil, for greasing

Mousse:	Mousse:
200 g plain chocolate, broken into pieces	7 oz plain chocolate, broken into pieces
4 × 15 ml spoons strong black coffee	4 tablespoons strong black coffee
25 g unsalted butter	1 oz unsalted butter
4 eggs, separated, whites stiffly beaten	4 eggs, separated, whites stiffly beaten
1–2 × 15 ml spoons vanilla sugar	1–2 tablespoons vanilla sugar
175 ml double or whipping cream, whipped	6 fl oz double or whipping cream, whipped
grated chocolate	grated chocolate

Preparation time: 40 minutes, plus overnight chilling
Cooking time: about 3¼ hours
Oven: 110°C, 225°F, Gas Mark ¼

In a mixing bowl, add the sugar to the beaten egg whites, a little at a time, beating well after each addition. Shape the meringue to line 4 shallow, lightly oiled 10–13 cm/4–5 inch ovenproof dishes, leaving a hollow in the middle. Bake the meringue cases in a preheated oven for 3 hours or until they are dry and crisp. Remove from the oven to cool.
Stir the chocolate pieces with the coffee in a saucepan over a low heat. Continue stirring until the chocolate melts and forms a smooth paste. Remove from the heat, stir in the butter, then the egg yolks, 1 at a time, and continue stirring until the mixture is smooth and glossy. Add the vanilla sugar to taste and mix well.
Add a spoonful of the chocolate mixture to the beaten egg whites and whisk gently to blend the ingredients. Carefully fold this mixture into the chocolate and pour the mousse into a bowl. Chill for at least 12 hours or overnight.
Just before serving, either fill the meringue cases with the mousse and serve in the dishes or unmould the meringue cases and spoon some of the mousse into each one. Decorate each with the whipped cream and grated chocolate.

Striped Bavarian cream; Coffee-chocolate mousse; Chocolate blancmange

Chocolate blancmange

Preparation time: 15 minutes, plus chilling
Cooking time: 15 minutes

Metric
250 ml milk
100 g plain chocolate,
　broken into pieces
65 g caster sugar
40 g vanilla sugar
1 × 2.5 ml spoon grated
　orange rind
20 g powdered gelatine
3 × 15 ml spoons cold
　water
500 ml double or whipping
　cream, lightly whipped
oil

Imperial
8 fl oz milk
4 oz plain chocolate,
　broken into pieces
2 ½ oz caster sugar
1 ½ oz vanilla sugar
½ teaspoon grated
　orange rind
¾ oz powdered gelatine
3 tablespoons cold
　water
18 fl oz double or whipping
　cream, lightly whipped
oil

Topping:
250 ml double or whipping
　cream, whipped
grated chocolate

Topping:
8 fl oz double or whipping
　cream, whipped
grated chocolate

Combine the milk with the chocolate pieces, sugars and orange rind in a saucepan. Stir constantly over a low heat, until the chocolate has melted and the mixture is smooth.

Leave the gelatine with the water in a small saucepan to soften. Set the pan over a low heat to dissolve the gelatine, then pour it into the chocolate mixture. Leave the mixture to cool to room temperature, stirring occasionally, then gently fold in the cream. Pour the mixture into a lightly oiled 1.2 litre/2 pint mould or dish and chill until set, or overnight. Unmould the blancmange and decorate with whipped cream and grated chocolate.

Serves 6

53

Spiced chocolate cream

Metric
500 ml milk
½ vanilla pod, split
1 × 2.5 ml spoon ground
 cinnamon
1 × 1.25 ml spoon ground
 nutmeg
pinch of ground allspice
100 g plain chocolate,
 broken into pieces
3 eggs, separated, whites
 stiffly beaten
90 g sugar
1 × 15 ml spoon powdered
 gelatine
3 × 15 ml spoons cold
 water
oil
whipped cream, to serve
 (optional)

Imperial
18 fl oz milk
½ vanilla pod, split
½ teaspoon ground
 cinnamon
¼ teaspoon ground
 nutmeg
pinch of ground allspice
4 oz plain chocolate,
 broken into pieces
3 eggs, separated, whites
 stiffly beaten
3½ oz sugar
1 tablespoon powdered
 gelatine
3 tablespoons cold
 water
oil
whipped cream, to serve
 (optional)

Preparation time: 30 minutes, plus infusing and chilling
Cooking time: about 25 minutes

Heat the milk in a saucepan to boiling point. Add the vanilla pod, cinnamon, nutmeg and allspice. Cover and remove from the heat. Leave to infuse for 30 minutes, then strain the milk into a bowl.

Place the chocolate pieces in a pan over a low heat, with enough of the infused milk to cover. Stir constantly as the chocolate melts and forms a smooth paste, then gradually add the remaining milk.

Whisk the egg yolks with the sugar in a mixing bowl, until the mixture falls off the whisk in a ribbon. Gradually pour in the milk, gently whisk the mixture, then pour back into the saucepan.

Leave the gelatine with the water in a small saucepan to soften. Set the pan over a low heat to dissolve the gelatine, then pour it into the saucepan with the chocolate mixture. Stir the custard over a low heat until it coats the back of the spoon. Remove from the heat and chill the mixture, stirring occasionally, until it begins to set. Gently fold a third of the beaten egg whites into the custard and then the rest. Pour the mixture into a lightly oiled 1 litre/1¾ pint mould. Chill until firm, or overnight. Unmould and for a richer dessert serve with whipped cream.
Serves 8

Custard creams

Metric
250 ml milk
1 vanilla pod
175 g plain chocolate,
    broken into pieces
6 egg yolks
300 ml double or whipping
    cream, whipped

Imperial
8 fl oz milk
1 vanilla pod
6 oz plain chocolate,
    broken into pieces
6 egg yolks
½ pint double or whipping
    cream, whipped

Preparation time: 30 minutes, plus infusing and cooling
Cooking time: 10–15 minutes

Bring the milk with the vanilla pod just to the boil in a saucepan. Remove from the heat and leave to infuse for 15 minutes. Remove the vanilla pod. Melt the chocolate with the milk over a low heat, stirring constantly until the mixture is smooth. Add the egg yolks and beat well. Cook the custard, stirring constantly until thick and smooth. Remove from the heat and leave to cool, stirring occasionally. To speed the cooling, place the pan in a bowl of cold water and continue stirring. Pour the custard into 6 small ramekins. Decorate the top of each with some of the whipped cream. Serve warm or cold.
Serves 6

From the left: Spiced chocolate cream;
Oeufs à la neige; Custard creams

Oeufs à la neige

Metric
6 eggs, separated, whites
    stiffly beaten
375 g caster sugar
600 ml milk
50 g plain chocolate,
    melted
25–50 g crushed Praline
    (page 44), to
    decorate

Imperial
6 eggs, separated, whites
    stiffly beaten
13 oz caster sugar
1 pint milk
2 oz plain chocolate,
    melted
1–2 oz crushed Praline
    (page 44), to
    decorate

Preparation time: 30 minutes
Cooking time: 15–20 minutes

Add 250 g/9 oz of the sugar, a little at a time, to the beaten egg whites, beating well after each addition. Heat the milk with 50 g/2 oz of the remaining sugar in a wide shallow pan to just below boiling point. Scoop up a tablespoonful of the meringue mixture and slide it on to the milk. Poach several meringues at a time for 3 minutes or until firm, turning them over once. With a slotted spoon, remove the meringues to a cloth to drain. Continue poaching the meringues in batches until all the mixture is used. Strain the milk into a bowl.
Whisk the egg yolks with the rest of the sugar until the mixture falls off the whisk in a ribbon. Stir the milk into the egg mixture, transfer to a heavy saucepan and cook over a low heat, until the custard coats the back of the spoon. Stir in the melted chocolate.
Pour the custard into a bowl and gently layer the meringues on the surface. Decorate the meringues with the crushed praline. Serve warm or cold.

Chocolate charlotte mousse

Metric
about 24 sponge finger
  biscuits
225 g plain chocolate,
  broken into pieces
65 ml strong black coffee
225 g unsalted butter,
  softened
75 g sugar
40 g vanilla sugar
3 eggs, separated, whites
  stiffly beaten
100 g whole almonds,
  lightly roasted and
  ground
250 ml double or whipping
  cream, whipped
double or whipping cream,
  whipped, to decorate
roasted almond flakes
  (optional)

Imperial
about 24 sponge finger
  biscuits
8 oz plain chocolate,
  broken into pieces
2 ½ fl oz strong black coffee
8 oz unsalted butter,
  softened
3 oz sugar
1 ½ oz vanilla sugar
3 eggs, separated, whites
  stiffly beaten
4 oz whole almonds,
  lightly roasted and
  ground
8 fl oz double or whipping
  cream, whipped
double or whipping cream,
  whipped, to decorate
roasted almond flakes
  (optional)

Preparation time: 20 minutes, plus setting
Cooking time: 10–15 minutes

Line the bottom of a 1.2 litre/2 pint charlotte mould with greaseproof paper. Stir the chocolate pieces with the coffee in a saucepan over a low heat. Continue stirring until the chocolate melts and forms a smooth paste. Remove from the heat and leave to cool slightly. Beat the butter with the sugars in a mixing bowl, until light and fluffy. Add the egg yolks, 1 at a time, beating well after each addition. Stir in the melted chocolate and the almonds. Gently fold a third of the beaten egg white into the chocolate mixture, then fold in the rest. Carefully fold in the whipped cream.
Line the sides of the prepared mould with sponge fingers, using some of the mousse to position them. Pour the mixture into the mould and chill for 4–5 hours, or overnight, until set. When set, turn out on to a serving plate and remove the greaseproof paper. Decorate with whipped cream and (if using) the almond flakes.
Serves 6–8

Petits pots de crème

Metric
600 ml milk
50 g roasted coffee
  beans, crushed
½ vanilla pod, split or
  1.25 ml spoon vanilla
  essence
75 g sugar
2 × 15 ml spoons cold
  water
3 × 15 ml spoons hot
  water
100 g plain chocolate,
  broken into pieces
5 egg yolks
1 whole egg

Imperial
1 pint milk
2 oz roasted coffee
  beans, crushed
½ vanilla pod, split or ¼
  teaspoon vanilla
  essence
3 oz sugar
2 tablespoons cold
  water
3 tablespoons hot
  water
4 oz plain chocolate,
  broken into pieces
5 egg yolks
1 whole egg

Preparation time: 15 minutes, plus infusing and chilling
Cooking time: about 40 minutes
Oven: 180°C, 350°F, Gas Mark 4

Heat the milk in a saucepan to boiling point. Add the coffee beans and the vanilla pod or essence, cover and remove from the heat. Leave to infuse for 15 minutes, then strain the milk into a bowl.
Combine the sugar and cold water in a heavy saucepan, stirring constantly over a medium heat, until all the sugar has dissolved. Bring the syrup to the boil and cook to a light golden caramel. Dip the base of the pan in cold water to arrest further cooking and add the hot water, return to a low heat and stir until it becomes a smooth syrup. Reserve.
Place the chocolate pieces in a pan with enough of the infused milk to cover, over a low heat, and stir constantly as the chocolate melts and forms a smooth paste, then gradually add the remaining milk. Stir in the caramel syrup.
Whisk the egg yolks and whole egg together in a mixing bowl until smooth. Gradually pour in the chocolate milk, gently whisking with the eggs. Spoon off the froth on the surface and pour the custard into 6 'petit pots' or small ramekins.
Place in a wide, deep casserole and pour in hot water to two-thirds of the depth of the ramekins. Cover the casserole and bake in a preheated oven for 20 minutes or until they are firm, but still tremble. Remove from the oven, leave the ramekins to cool for a few minutes in the hot water, then remove and chill.
Makes 6

Chocolate charlotte mousse; Petits pots de crème

FROZEN DESSERTS

Frozen chocolate desserts are among the
greatest pleasures of summer. This chapter
contains three basic chocolate ice creams, which
are also used in combination with other
ingredients, such as fruit, meringue, chestnut
and sponge, as well as frozen soufflés and mousse
mixtures. An electric churn and a freezer make
the process of ice cream making simpler but
the freezing compartment of a refrigerator,
provided it has a 3 star marking, can be used. Ice
creams should be softened before serving. To
do this, leave them to stand in the refrigerator for
30 minutes.

Baked Alaska

Metric
about 2 quantities
  Chocolate Ice Cream
  (page 64)
1 chocolate sponge sheet
  (page 13)
3 egg whites
120 g caster sugar

Imperial
about 2 quantities
  Chocolate Ice Cream
  (page 64)
1 chocolate sponge sheet
  (page 13)
3 egg whites
4 ½ oz caster sugar

Preparation time: 30 minutes, plus freezing
Cooking time: 5 minutes
Oven: 230°C, 450°F, Gas Mark 8

The sponge sheet is made as described for the Chocolate Swiss Roll with Truffles. Any trimmings can be used up in the Raspberry Bombe (page 65).

Place the ice cream in a 450 g/1 lb loaf tin lined with greaseproof paper and freeze. Cut the sponge sheet slightly larger than the mould and turn the block of ice cream out on to it. Place in the freezer while preparing the meringue.
Whisk the egg whites to stiff peaks and add the sugar, a little at a time, beating well after each addition, until the meringue is stiff.
Remove the ice cream from the freezer, place on an ovenproof dish and remove the greaseproof paper. Completely cover the ice cream and sponge with the meringue and bake in a preheated oven for 5 minutes or until the meringue is lightly browned. Remove from the oven and serve immediately.
Serves 6–8

Double chocolate chip ice cream

Metric
90 g plain chocolate,
  broken into pieces
300 ml milk
3 egg yolks
75 g sugar
300 ml double or whipping
  cream, whipped
65 g chopped chocolate

Imperial
3 ½ oz plain chocolate,
  broken into pieces
½ pint milk
3 egg yolks
3 oz sugar
½ pint double or whipping
  cream, whipped
2 ½ oz chopped chocolate

Preparation time: 10 minutes, plus freezing
Cooking time: about 15 minutes

Stir the chocolate pieces with the milk in a saucepan over a low heat, until the chocolate melts and the mixture is smooth. Whisk the egg yolks with the sugar in a mixing bowl, until the mixture falls off the whisk in a thick ribbon. Gradually add the chocolate-flavoured milk, whisking constantly. Pour the mixture back into the saucepan and stir over a medium heat, until it thickens and coats the back of the spoon. Strain into a bowl and cool in the refrigerator or stir over a bowl of ice. When cold, fold in the whipped cream.
If churning the ice cream, pour the mixture into the churn, add the chopped chocolate and follow the manufacturer's instructions. If using ice trays, pour the mixture into the trays and freeze until the ice cream begins to set around the edges. Pour into a mixing bowl, add the chopped chocolate and whisk until the ice cream is smooth. Return to the trays and freeze for 30 minutes.
Repeat whisking and freezing at 30 minute intervals until the ice cream thickens, then leave until set.
Serves 6–8

Baked Alaska; Double chocolate chip ice cream

Frozen chocolate soufflé

Metric	Imperial
3 eggs, separated, whites stiffly beaten	3 eggs, separated, whites stiffly beaten
50 g sugar	2 oz sugar
90 g plain chocolate, melted and cooled	3½ oz plain chocolate, melted and cooled
350 ml double cream, whipped	12 fl oz double cream, whipped
chocolate scrolls	chocolate scrolls
icing sugar	icing sugar

Preparation time: 25 minutes, plus freezing
Cooking time: 10–15 minutes

This delicious chocolate cream appears to rise like a baked soufflé, making an attractive finish to a meal.

Wrap and secure a collar of greaseproof paper around a 600 ml/1 pint soufflé dish to stand 5 cm/2 inches above the rim.
Whisk the egg yolks and sugar in a heatproof bowl placed over a pan of barely simmering water, until the sugar is dissolved and the mixture falls off the whisk in a thick ribbon. Remove from the heat and whisk in the melted chocolate. Continue whisking until cool, fold in the cream, then gently fold in the beaten egg whites. Pour into the dish and freeze for at least 4 hours. Just before serving remove the paper collar, decorate the top with the chocolate scrolls and dust lightly with icing sugar.
Serves 6

Poires belle-hélène

Metric	Imperial
150 g caster sugar	5 oz caster sugar
1 vanilla pod	1 vanilla pod
6 pears, peeled, halved and cored	6 pears, peeled, halved and cored
Chocolate Ice Cream (page 64)	Chocolate Ice Cream (page 64)
Chocolate Butter Sauce (page 68)	Chocolate Butter Sauce (page 68)

Preparation time: 10 minutes, plus cooling
Cooking time: 10–20 minutes

Place the sugar, vanilla pod and pear halves in a large saucepan and add enough water just to cover. Simmer gently for 10–20 minutes or until tender. Leave the pears to cool in the syrup.
To serve, place 1 or 2 scoops of chocolate ice cream in individual chilled dessert bowls. Arrange 2 pear halves on top and pour over the hot chocolate butter sauce. Serve immediately.
Serves 6

Chocolate ice box cake

Preparation time: 1 hour, plus freezing
Cooking time: 40–45 minutes
Oven: 190°C, 375°F, Gas Mark 5

Metric
butter, for greasing
7 eggs, separated, whites
    stiffly beaten
75 g vanilla sugar
5 × 15 ml spoons plain
    flour, sifted
pinch of salt
caster sugar

Filling:
350 g plain chocolate,
    broken into pieces
2 × 15 ml spoons strong
    black coffee
50 ml brandy
2 egg yolks
5 egg whites, stiffly beaten
120 ml double or whipping
    cream, whipped

Icing:
150 ml double cream
150 g plain chocolate,
    broken into pieces

Imperial
butter, for greasing
7 eggs, separated, whites
    stiffly beaten
3 oz vanilla sugar
5 tablespoons plain
    flour, sifted
pinch of salt
caster sugar

Filling:
12 oz plain chocolate,
    broken into pieces
2 tablespoons strong black
    coffee
2 fl oz brandy
2 egg yolks
5 egg whites, stiffly beaten
4 fl oz double or whipping
    cream, whipped

Icing:
¼ pint double cream
5 oz plain chocolate,
    broken into pieces

Frozen chocolate soufflé; Poires belle-hélène with
Chocolate butter sauce; Chocolate ice box cake

Butter and line two 23 × 30 cm/9 × 12 inch Swiss roll tins with greaseproof paper. Brush with melted butter and dust with flour. Whisk the egg yolks with the sugar in a mixing bowl, until the mixture falls off the whisk in a thick ribbon. Fold in the flour and salt. Gently fold in a third of the beaten egg whites, then fold in the rest. Divide the mixture evenly between the tins and bake in a preheated oven for 15–20 minutes or until lightly golden on top.

Spread 2 kitchen towels on a work surface, cover them with greaseproof paper and sprinkle the paper with caster sugar. When cooked, turn the sponges out upside down on to the sugared paper. Peel off the greaseproof paper used to line the tin and leave to cool. Using the base of a 20 cm/8 inch spring-form cake tin as a guide, cut a circle of cake from each sponge sheet. Line the bottom of the cake tin with a circle of greaseproof paper and cover with a sponge circle. Cut 3 strips from the remainder of the sponge sheets, about 5 cm/2 inches wide, to line the sides of the tin.

To make the filling, put the chocolate pieces, coffee and brandy in a saucepan over a low heat and stir constantly as the chocolate melts, until the mixture forms a smooth paste. Remove from the heat and leave to cool slightly. Beat in the egg yolks, 1 at a time, and continue stirring until the mixture is smooth. Gently fold in a third of the beaten egg whites, then fold in the rest. Fold in the whipped cream.

Pour the mixture into the lined cake tin, place the remaining sponge circle on top, and cover with a weighted 20 cm/8 inch cake tin. Place in the freezer for 2 hours or refrigerate for at least 5 hours.

To make the icing, pour the cream into a saucepan and bring just to the boil. Stir in the chocolate pieces and continue stirring as the chocolate melts, until the mixture is thick and smooth. When the cake is set, remove the sides and base of the tin. Pour over the icing and return to the refrigerator or freezer.

Makes one 20 cm/8 inch cake

Icebox cake with bourbon

Metric
butter, for greasing
4 eggs, separated, whites
  stiffly beaten
100 g sugar
40 g cocoa powder, sifted
40 g plain flour
pinch of salt
caster sugar

Filling:
1 quantity Double
  Chocolate Chip Ice
  Cream (page 59)
50 ml bourbon
icing sugar, to decorate
Chocolate Butter Sauce
  (page 68), to serve

Imperial
butter, for greasing
4 eggs, separated, whites
  stiffly beaten
4 oz sugar
1½ oz cocoa powder, sifted
1½ oz plain flour
pinch of salt
caster sugar

Filling:
1 quantity Double
  Chocolate Chip Ice
  Cream (page 59)
2 fl oz bourbon
icing sugar, to decorate
Chocolate Butter Sauce
  (page 68), to serve

Preparation time: 30 minutes, plus freezing
Cooking time: 10–12 minutes
Oven: 190°C, 375°F, Gas Mark 5

Butter and line a 23 × 33 cm/9 × 13 inch Swiss roll tin with greaseproof paper. Brush with melted butter and dust with flour. Whisk the egg yolks with the sugar in a mixing bowl, until the mixture falls off the whisk in a thick ribbon. Sift together the cocoa powder, flour and salt, then fold into the egg yolks. Gently fold in a third of the beaten egg whites, then fold in the rest. Spread the mixture into the tin smoothly and bake in a pre-heated oven for 10–12 minutes or until springy to the touch.

Spread a kitchen towel on a work surface, cover it with greaseproof paper and sprinkle with caster sugar. When cooked, turn the sponge out upside down on to the sugared paper. Peel off the greaseproof paper used to line the tin.

Trim the edges of the sponge and make a shallow groove along 1 short side of the cake 2.5 cm/1 inch from the edge. Cover the sponge with greaseproof paper. Fold the sponge over at the groove. Using the towel to support the cake, roll it up and cover with a damp cloth until cool.

Leave the chocolate chip ice cream to soften in the refrigerator for about 30 minutes. Unroll the sponge, remove the greaseproof paper and brush with the bourbon. Spread the sponge with a layer of the softened ice cream and roll it up. Place on a platter and freeze for at least 4 hours.

Just before serving, dust the cake with icing sugar. Cut the cake into slices and serve with chocolate butter sauce.

Makes one 23 cm/9 inch cake

Chocolate chestnut bombe

Metric
1 quantity Double
  Chocolate Chip Ice
  Cream (page 59),
  slightly softened

Filling:
350 g chestnuts, shells slit
300 ml milk
1 vanilla pod
100–175 g caster sugar
2 egg yolks
300 ml double or whipping
  cream, lightly whipped
1 egg white, stiffly beaten

Imperial
1 quantity Double
  Chocolate Chip Ice
  Cream (page 59),
  slightly softened

Filling:
12 oz chestnuts, shells slit
½ pint milk
1 vanilla pod
4–6 oz caster sugar
2 egg yolks
½ pint double or whipping
  cream, lightly whipped
1 egg white, stiffly beaten

Preparation time: 50 minutes, plus freezing
Cooking time: 55 minutes

Chill a 1.5 litre/2½ pint bombe mould in the freezer, then line with the softened ice cream, smoothing it to make a neat cavity. Return to the freezer.

To make the filling, drop the chestnuts into boiling water and parboil them for 10 minutes. Remove from the heat. Lift out the chestnuts a few at a time, leaving the rest to soak, cut away the shells and peel away the skins. Put the chestnuts in a pan with the milk, vanilla pod and 65 g/2½ oz of the sugar. Bring to the boil, then cover and reduce the heat. Simmer for about 45 minutes or until tender.

Remove the vanilla pod. Strain the chestnuts, reserving the milk, and purée through a sieve or a food mill. The purée should be a smooth, moist paste; if too dry, add a little of the reserved milk. Stir in the remaining sugar to taste and beat in the egg yolks. Leave to cool. Gently fold in the whipped cream, then fold in the beaten egg white.

Fill the mould with the chestnut filling, place a round of greaseproof paper on top and cover with the lid. Freeze for about 4 hours.

To unmould, remove the lid and greaseproof paper, place mould in warm water for one minute, then invert it on to a chilled serving plate. Remove the mould and leave the bombe to soften in the refrigerator for 15–30 minutes before serving.

Serves 8

Icebox cake with bourbon; Chocolate chestnut bombe; Rum-flavoured chocolate parfait

Rum-flavoured chocolate parfait

Metric
100 g sugar
120 ml water
100 g plain chocolate,
  broken into pieces
4 egg yolks
1 × 15 ml spoon strong
  black coffee
1 × 15 ml spoon rum
300 ml double cream,
  lightly whipped

Imperial
4 oz sugar
4 fl oz water
4 oz plain chocolate,
  broken into pieces
4 egg yolks
1 tablespoon strong black
  coffee
1 tablespoon rum
½ pint double cream,
  lightly whipped

Preparation time: 35 minutes, plus freezing
Cooking time: 15–20 minutes

If you have the type of glass which will go in the freezer, you can pour the mixture straight into the glasses and freeze until ready to serve.

Stir the sugar with the water in a saucepan over a low heat, until the sugar is dissolved. Bring the syrup to the boil and cook for 3 minutes. Remove from the heat, add the chocolate and stir until the chocolate melts and the mixture is smooth. Leave the syrup to cool.

Whisk the egg yolks in a heatproof mixing bowl, until they are light and fluffy. Gradually pour in the reserved syrup, whisking continuously. Add the coffee and rum, place the bowl in a water bath of barely simmering water, whisking continuously, until the mixture falls off the whisk in a thick ribbon. Place the bowl over ice and whisk until the mixture is cool. Gently fold in the cream. Pour the chocolate cream into a freezer container. Cover, seal and freeze. Before serving, allow to soften, then scoop into individual dishes or parfait glasses.

Bitter chocolate ice

Metric	Imperial
600 ml milk	1 pint milk
150 g caster sugar	5 oz caster sugar
100 g plain chocolate, broken into pieces	4 oz plain chocolate, broken into pieces
75 g cocoa powder	3 oz cocoa powder
300 ml double or whipping cream, whipped	½ pint double or whipping cream, whipped

Preparation time: 15 minutes, plus freezing
Cooking time: 10–15 minutes

Put the milk and sugar in a saucepan and bring just to the boil. Add the chocolate pieces and stir until the chocolate melts and the mixture is smooth. Whisk in the cocoa powder until thoroughly blended. Strain the mixture into a bowl and leave to cool, stirring occasionally, then gently fold in the whipped cream. Pour the chocolate mixture into a churn or into ice trays. If using a churn, follow the manufacturer's instructions. If using ice trays, after freezing for 30 minutes, stir the frozen edges of the mixture into the centre, breaking up any large crystals as you do so. Repeat this procedure every hour until the ice is set in small light crystals.
Serves 8

Chocolate ice cream

Metric	Imperial
100 g plain chocolate, broken into pieces	4 oz plain chocolate, broken into pieces
600 ml milk	1 pint milk
7 egg yolks	7 egg yolks
100 g sugar	4 oz sugar

Preparation time: 10 minutes, plus freezing
Cooking time: 15–20 minutes

In a saucepan over a low heat, stir the chocolate pieces with just enough of the milk to cover the bottom of the pan. Stir continuously as the chocolate melts, until the mixture forms a smooth paste, then gradually stir in the remaining milk.
Whisk the egg yolks with the sugar in a mixing bowl, until the mixture falls off the whisk in a thick ribbon. Gradually add the chocolate-flavoured milk, whisking constantly. Pour back into the saucepan and stir over a medium heat, until the mixture thickens and coats the back of the spoon. Strain into a bowl and cool in the refrigerator or stir over a bowl of ice.
Pour into a churn or into ice trays. If using a churn, follow the manufacturer's instructions for churning the ice cream. If using ice trays, pour the mixture into the trays and freeze until the ice cream begins to set around the edges. Pour into a mixing bowl and whisk until smooth. Return to the trays and freeze for 30 minutes. Repeat whisking and freezing at 30 minute intervals until the ice cream is thick and smooth, then freeze until ready to serve.
Serves 6–8

Raspberry bombe

Preparation time: 40 minutes, plus freezing
Cooking time: 10–15 minutes

Metric
about 1 quantity
Chocolate Ice Cream
(page 64), slightly
softened

Imperial
about 1 quantity
Chocolate Ice Cream
(page 64), slightly
softened

Filling:
3 egg yolks
90 g caster sugar
2 × 15 ml spoons Kirsch
1 × 15 ml spoon lemon
    juice
50 g stale chocolate cake
    crumbs or stale
    pumpernickel, finely
    ground
400 g raspberries
150 ml double or whipping
    cream, whipped
1 egg white, stiffly beaten
double or whipping cream,
    whipped, to decorate

Filling:
3 egg yolks
3½ oz caster sugar
2 tablespoons Kirsch
1 tablespoon lemon
    juice
2 oz stale chocolate cake
    crumbs or stale
    pumpernickel, finely
    ground
14 oz raspberries
¼ pint double or whipping
    cream, whipped
1 egg white, stiffly beaten
double or whipping cream,
    whipped, to decorate

Chill a 1.2 litre/2 pint bombe mould in the freezer, then line with the softened ice cream, smoothing it to make a neat cavity. Return to the freezer.

To make the filling, whisk the egg yolks and sugar in a heatproof bowl placed over a pan of barely simmering water, until the sugar is dissolved and the mixture falls off the whisk in a thick ribbon. Remove from the heat, place the bowl over ice and beat until cool. Beat in the Kirsch, lemon juice and cake crumbs or pumpernickel. Reserve a few raspberries for decoration and fold in the rest, then the whipped cream, and gently fold in the beaten egg white.

Fill the mould with the raspberry mixture, place a round of greaseproof paper on top and cover with the lid. Freeze for about 4 hours.

To unmould, remove the lid and greaseproof paper, place mould in warm water for one minute, then invert it on to a chilled serving plate. Remove the mould, decorate with whipped cream and raspberries, and leave to soften in the refrigerator for 15–30 minutes before serving.

Serves 8

From the left: Chocolate ice cream; Bitter chocolate ice; Raspberry bombe

DRINKS AND SAUCES

This section features two hot drinks, including an adaptation of the original Aztec recipe and one refreshing iced cup for summer. Of the five sauces, the chocolate fudge is a traditional sauce for vanilla ice cream, whereas the custard sauce provides a simple accompaniment to many of the chocolate desserts. All the drinks and sauces are simply made by heating together different ingredients.

Iced chocolate

Metric	Imperial
175 g sugar	6 oz sugar
200 ml water	1/3 pint water
40 g cocoa powder	1 1/2 oz cocoa powder
milk	milk

Preparation time: 5 minutes, plus chilling
Cooking time: 15 minutes

The chocolate syrup can be stored in the refrigerator and used when required.

Place the sugar and water in a heavy saucepan and stir over a medium heat until all the sugar dissolves. Brush away any sugar crystals that have formed on the side of the pan with a pastry brush dipped in cold water. Increase the heat and bring the syrup to the boil. Cook the syrup to 102°C/215°F, or until the syrup spins a short, fine thread from the spoon. Remove the pan from the heat. Add the cocoa powder and stir until well mixed over a low heat for 2 minutes. Leave the syrup to cool and refrigerate.
Add 1 × 15 ml spoon/1 tablespoon chilled syrup for each 300 ml/½ pint of milk and stir until blended. Pour the chocolate over ice into chilled glasses.
Makes 150 ml/¼ pint chocolate syrup

Spiced chocolate cup

Metric	Imperial
600 ml milk	1 pint milk
300 ml double cream	½ pint double cream
pinch of salt	pinch of salt
1 × 2.5 ml spoon ground nutmeg	½ teaspoon ground nutmeg
pinch of ground allspice	pinch of ground allspice
1 × 2.5 ml spoon ground cinnamon	½ teaspoon ground cinnamon
50 g plain chocolate	2 oz plain chocolate
85 ml water	3 fl oz water
2 egg yolks	2 egg yolks

Preparation time: 20 minutes
Cooking time: about 1¼ hours

This thick, spiced beverage is adapted from the ancient Aztec drink 'xocoatl'. You can, if you like, add vanilla sugar.

Bring the milk and cream just to the boil in the top of a double boiler, add the salt, nutmeg, allspice and cinnamon and reduce the heat. Cook at a bare simmer for 1 hour.
Melt the chocolate with the water in a small saucepan over a gentle heat. Remove from the heat and whisk the mixture to a paste. Beat in the egg yolks and stir into the milk and spice mixture. Continue stirring until the mixture thickens. Pour the spiced chocolate into small cups and serve immediately.
Serves 6

French chocolate

Metric	Imperial
175 g plain chocolate, broken into pieces	6 oz plain chocolate, broken into pieces
175 ml hot water	6 fl oz hot water
450 ml milk	¾ pint milk

Preparation time: 5 minutes
Cooking time: 5 minutes

Thicker than hot chocolate, this beverage in Spain is served with Churros (page 40) for breakfast.

In a saucepan, melt the chocolate with the hot water, whisking until the mixture thickens. Heat the milk in another saucepan. Divide the melted chocolate between 4 hot mugs and, without stirring, fill each with the hot milk. Serve immediately.

Custard sauce

Metric	Imperial
600 ml milk	1 pint milk
6 egg yolks	6 egg yolks
50 g caster sugar	2 oz caster sugar

Preparation time: 5 minutes
Cooking time: 15–20 minutes

Bring the milk just to the boil in a saucepan, then remove from the heat. Whisk the egg yolks and sugar together in a mixing bowl, until the mixture falls off the whisk in a thick ribbon. Gradually pour in the milk, whisking all the time. Pour the mixture back into the saucepan and stir over a low heat until it coats the back of the spoon. Remove from the heat, dip the base of the pan in cold water to arrest further cooking and stir the custard until it cools slightly. Strain and serve hot or cold.
Makes 600 ml/1 pint

From the left: Iced chocolate; Spiced chocolate cup; French chocolate; Custard sauce

Chocolate fudge sauce

Metric
50 g plain chocolate,
  broken into pieces
40 g unsalted butter
1 ½ × 15 ml spoons liquid
  glucose
85 ml boiling water
25 ml strong black
  coffee
150 g sugar
50 g vanilla sugar
pinch of salt

Imperial
2 oz plain chocolate,
  broken into pieces
1 ½ oz unsalted butter
1 ½ tablespoons liquid
  glucose
3 fl oz boiling water
1 fl oz strong black
  coffee
5 oz sugar
2 oz vanilla sugar
pinch of salt

Cooking time: 15 minutes

This sweet sauce goes well with vanilla ice cream.

Place all the ingredients in a saucepan over a low heat and stir until the chocolate melts and the mixture is smooth. Bring to the boil and cook for 3 minutes. Serve hot or warm.
Makes 350 ml/12 fl oz

Chocolate butter sauce

Metric
225 g plain chocolate,
  broken into pieces
250 ml water
1 × 15 ml spoon brandy or
  rum (optional)
90 g unsalted butter, cut
  into pieces

Imperial
8 oz plain chocolate,
  broken into pieces
8 fl oz water
1 tablespoon brandy or
  rum (optional)
3 ½ oz unsalted butter, cut
  into pieces

Preparation time: 5 minutes
Cooking time: 10 minutes

Stir the chocolate pieces, water and, if using, the brandy or rum together in a saucepan over a low heat, until the chocolate melts and the mixture is smooth. Remove from the heat and gradually stir in the butter, until it melts and the sauce is glossy. Serve hot or cold.
Makes 450 ml/¾ pint

Chocolate cream sauce

Metric
300 ml double cream
1 × 15 ml spoon brandy
(optional)
1 × 15 ml spoon strong
black coffee (optional)
225 g plain chocolate,
broken into pieces

Imperial
½ pint double cream
1 tablespoon brandy
(optional)
1 tablespoon strong
black coffee (optional)
8 oz plain chocolate,
broken into pieces

Preparation time: 5 minutes
Cooking time: 10–15 minutes

Pour the cream and, if using, the brandy and coffee, into a saucepan and bring just to the boil. Add the chocolate pieces and stir until the chocolate melts and the mixture is smooth. Serve hot or cold.
Makes 450 ml/¾ pint

Bittersweet chocolate sauce

Metric
120 ml double cream
2 × 15 ml spoons strong
black coffee
100 g plain chocolate,
broken into pieces
85 ml apricot jam

Imperial
4 fl oz double cream
2 tablespoons strong
black coffee
4 oz plain chocolate,
broken into pieces
3 fl oz apricot jam

Cooking time: 15 minutes

Put all the ingredients in a saucepan and stir constantly over a low heat, until the mixture is smooth and evenly blended. For a smoother sauce, press through a fine sieve. Serve hot or warm.
Makes about 250 ml/8 fl oz

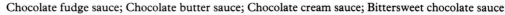

Chocolate fudge sauce; Chocolate butter sauce; Chocolate cream sauce; Bittersweet chocolate sauce

CONFECTIONERY AND BISCUITS

The skills required to make chocolate biscuits and confectionery range from the simple whisked paste, which is used in truffles, spirals and praline log, to the more involved sugar syrup recipes, such as the orange squares and the syrup brownies. These latter require a sugar thermometer so that the syrup is both cooked and cooled to the correct temperature. All the recipes are rich-tasting, visually attractive accompaniments either to morning coffee or afternoon tea.

Cinnamon fudge

Metric	Imperial
750 g sugar	1 ½ lb sugar
300 ml milk	½ pint milk
120 g unsalted butter	4 ½ oz unsalted butter
175 g plain chocolate, broken into pieces	6 oz plain chocolate, broken into pieces
1 ½ × 5 ml spoons ground cinnamon	1 ½ teaspoons ground cinnamon

Preparation time: 10 minutes, plus cooling
Cooking time: 15–20 minutes

Put the sugar, milk, butter and chocolate into a heavy saucepan. Over a medium heat, stir constantly until the sugar has dissolved and both the butter and the chocolate have melted. Bring the mixture to the boil and cook it to the soft ball stage, 116°C/240°F.
Remove the pan from the heat and briefly dip its base in cold water to arrest further cooking. Add the cinnamon. Beat the mixture by hand for several minutes until it thickens and becomes lighter in colour.
Pour the mixture into a buttered 20 cm/8 inch square tin. Leave to set in a cool place for 1–2 hours. Cut the fudge into 2.5 cm/1 inch squares.
Makes 1 kg/2¼ lb

Dark diamonds

Metric	Imperial
2 egg yolks	2 egg yolks
75 g vanilla sugar	3 oz vanilla sugar
50 g unsalted butter, softened	2 oz unsalted butter, softened
50 ml double cream	2 fl oz double cream
juice of ½ orange	juice of ½ orange
1 × 2.5 ml spoon grated orange rind	½ teaspoon grated orange rind
225 g plain chocolate, broken into pieces	8 oz plain chocolate, broken into pieces
50 g chopped pecan or walnut halves	2 oz chopped pecan or walnut halves
175 g dipping or plain chocolate	6 oz dipping or plain chocolate

Preparation time: 15 minutes, plus setting
Cooking time: 20–25 minutes

This soft and nutty chocolate confection is served in paper cases.

Beat the egg yolks with the sugar in a saucepan until light and pale. Add the butter, cream, orange juice and orange rind to the egg mixture. Stir the mixture over a medium heat until thick, but do not allow to boil. Add the chocolate and the chopped pecans or walnuts and stir until the chocolate has melted. Pour the mixture into a 20 × 25 cm/8 × 10 inch tin lined with non-stick silicone paper. Allow the mixture to cool. When set, turn out, remove the paper and cut into diamond shapes.
Line a tray with non-stick silicone paper.
Melt the dipping or plain chocolate. With a dipping fork, dip one end of each diamond into the chocolate. Allow the excess to drip away and wipe the bottom of the fork on the bowl's edge. Let the diamond slide off the fork on to the paper to dry.
Makes about 450 g/1 lb

Cocoa meringues

Metric	Imperial
2 egg whites	2 egg whites
100 g caster sugar	4 oz caster sugar
2 × 5 ml spoons cocoa powder	2 teaspoons cocoa powder
oil, for greasing	oil, for greasing

Filling:	**Filling:**
120 ml double cream	4 fl oz double cream
1 ½ × 15 ml spoons caster sugar	1 ½ tablespoons caster sugar
2 × 5 ml spoons cocoa powder	2 teaspoons cocoa powder

Preparation time: 15 minutes, plus cooling
Cooking time: 3 hours
Oven: 110°C, 225°F, Gas Mark ¼

Beat the egg whites in a clean bowl until they form stiff peaks. Add the sugar, a little at a time, beating well after each addition. Continue to beat until stiff and glossy. Gently fold in the cocoa powder.
Lightly oil a baking sheet and cover it with grease-proof paper. Spoon the cocoa meringue into a piping bag fitted with a 1 cm/½ inch star nozzle and pipe the meringue into spirals, 4 cm/1½ inches in diameter, on to the baking sheet.
Bake the meringues in a preheated oven for 3 hours or until they are dry and can be easily detached from the greaseproof paper. Remove to a wire tray and leave until cool.
Whip the cream with the caster sugar in a cold bowl. Fold in the cocoa powder. Spoon the whipped cream over half the meringues and sandwich together with the remaining meringues.
Makes 12

Cinnamon fudge; Dark diamonds; Cocoa meringues

Truffles

Metric
350 g plain chocolate,
    broken into pieces
150 ml double cream
2–4 × 15 ml spoons
    brandy
cocoa powder
crushed Praline
    (page 44) or icing
    sugar, to decorate

Imperial
12 oz plain chocolate,
    broken into pieces
¼ pint double cream
2–4 tablespoons
    brandy
cocoa powder
crushed Praline
    (page 44) or icing
    sugar, to decorate

Preparation time: 20 minutes, plus cooling
Cooking time: 15–20 minutes

Melt the chocolate in a heatproof mixing bowl over
a pan of hot water, stirring occasionally until the
chocolate is smooth. Remove the bowl.
Warm the cream in a small saucepan until tepid, and
slowly pour it into the melted chocolate, stirring constantly. Leave the mixture to cool. Stir the brandy
(according to taste) into the chocolate. Vigorously
whisk the paste until it is lighter in colour and holds
soft peaks. Chill until firm enough to shape by hand.
Sift a layer of cocoa powder on to a work surface.
Using 1 teaspoon, spoon out enough paste to form
a 2.5 cm/1 inch ball. With another spoon push the
paste on to the cocoa powder. Shape each piece into
a ball. Alternatively, roll in the crushed praline or
icing sugar. Serve the truffles in paper cases.
Makes 30

Chocolate praline log

Metric
175 g plain chocolate
1 × 15 ml spoon strong
    black coffee
1 × 15 ml spoon brandy
    (optional)
25 g caster sugar
75 g unsalted butter
2 egg yolks
1 egg white, lightly beaten
150 g crushed Praline
    (page 44)

Imperial
6 oz plain chocolate
1 tablespoon strong
    black coffee
1 tablespoon brandy
    (optional)
1 oz caster sugar
3 oz unsalted butter
2 egg yolks
1 egg white, lightly beaten
5 oz crushed Praline
    (page 44)

Preparation time: 15 minutes, plus cooling
Cooking time: 15–20 minutes

Melt the chocolate in a heatproof bowl with the
coffee, brandy, sugar and butter over a medium heat.
Remove from the heat and leave to cool for several
minutes. Stir in the egg yolks well. Chill the chocolate
mixture for 3 hours or until firm enough to shape.
Shape into a log 5 cm/2 inches in diameter. Brush the
log with the beaten egg white. Roll the log in the
crushed praline, pressing gently with your hands.
Chill the log until firm enough to slice, 2–3 hours.
To serve, slice the praline log into 5 mm/¼ inch slices.
Makes 36 slices

Truffles; Chocolate praline log; Raisin and nut clusters; Chocolate orange fudge

Raisin and nut clusters

Metric	Imperial
225 g raisins	8 oz raisins
225 g hazelnuts, roasted and skinned	8 oz hazelnuts, roasted and skinned
75 g crushed Praline (page 44)	3 oz crushed Praline (page 44)
400 g plain chocolate, melted	14 oz plain chocolate, melted
350 g dipping or plain chocolate	12 oz dipping or plain chocolate

Preparation time: 30 minutes, plus setting

An all-time favourite that is easily made at home.

Combine the raisins, hazelnuts and crushed praline in a large bowl. Add the melted chocolate and stir the ingredients until thoroughly mixed.

Line a tray with non-stick silicone paper. To shape each cluster, take 1 teaspoonful of the mixture and, with the back of another teaspoon, push the cluster on to the non-stick silicone paper. Leave to set in a cool place for about 1 hour.

Line another tray with non-stick silicone paper. Melt the dipping or plain chocolate in a heatproof bowl. With a dipping fork, dip the clusters into the chocolate. Allow the excess to drip away and wipe the bottom of the fork on the bowl's edge. Let the clusters slide off the fork on to the wax paper to harden.

Place the clusters in paper cases to serve.

Makes 36

Chocolate orange fudge

Metric	Imperial
400 g sugar	14 oz sugar
200 ml milk	⅓ pint milk
75 g unsalted butter	3 oz unsalted butter
120 ml maple syrup	4 fl oz maple syrup
120 g plain chocolate, broken into pieces	4 ½ oz plain chocolate, broken into pieces
grated rind of 1 orange	grated rind of 1 orange

Preparation time: 10 minutes, plus cooling
Cooking time: 15–20 minutes

This is a smooth fudge that hints of maple and the sharpness of orange.

Combine all the ingredients in a heavy saucepan. Over a gentle heat, stir constantly until all the sugar has dissolved and the butter and chocolate have melted. Bring the mixture to the boil and cook it to the soft ball stage, 116°C/240°F.

Remove the pan from the heat and dip its base in cold water to arrest further cooking. Leave the mixture to cool to 43°C/110°F. Beat the cooled syrup until it just thickens and lightens in colour. Scrape the fudge into a buttered 20 cm/8 inch square tin. Smooth over to level the surface.

Leave to set in a cool place. When firm, cut the fudge into 2.5 cm/1 inch squares.

Makes 750 g/1¾ lb

Chocolate creams

Metric	Imperial
450 g sugar	1 lb sugar
150 ml water	¼ pint water
1 ½ × 15 ml spoons liquid glucose	1 ½ tablespoons liquid glucose
100 g plain chocolate, broken into pieces	4 oz plain chocolate, broken into pieces
2 × 15 ml spoons brandy	2 tablespoons brandy
30 almonds, roasted	30 almonds, roasted

Preparation time: 35 minutes, plus chilling overnight
Cooking time: 25–30 minutes

A rich, brandy-flavoured chocolate fondant which melts in the mouth.

Place the sugar, water and liquid glucose in a heavy saucepan and stir over a low to medium heat until the sugar dissolves. Brush away any sugar crystals that have formed on the sides of the pan with a pastry brush dipped in cold water. Increase the heat and bring the syrup to the boil. Cook the syrup to the soft ball stage, 116°C/240°F. Remove the pan from the heat straightaway and dip its base in cold water to arrest further cooking.
Lightly sprinkle a work surface with water. Pour the syrup on to the prepared work surface and leave to cool for several minutes. With a dampened metal scraper keep folding the edges of the syrup into the centre until glossy with a yellow tinge. Work the syrup in a figure-of-eight with a dampened wooden spatula until white and crumbly, about 5–10 minutes. With wet hands, gather the fondant into a ball and knead for about 10 mintues until it is smooth. Wrap in cling film or kitchen foil and chill overnight.
Place the fondant in a heatproof bowl in a pan of simmering water and stir as it melts. Add the chocolate pieces and brandy. Stir the mixture until the chocolate has melted and the fondant reaches a temperature of 60°C/140°F. Spoon the fondant into paper cases, pressing an almond into each one as you do so.
Makes 30

Variation:
The fondant described here may also be used for dipping or as icing for both cakes and pastries such as éclairs. If it is to be used for dipping, cook it to 113°C/236°F, or to 115°C/238°F for icing.

Meringue mushrooms

Metric	Imperial
4 egg whites	4 egg whites
225 g caster sugar	8 oz caster sugar
oil, for greasing	oil, for greasing
cocoa powder, for dusting	cocoa powder, for dusting
150 g plain chocolate, melted	5 oz plain chocolate, melted

Preparation time: 1 hour
Cooking time: 3 hours
Oven: 110°, 225°F, Gas Mark ¼

Beat the egg whites in a bowl until they form stiff peaks. Add the sugar a little at a time, beating well after each addition, until stiff and firm.
Lightly oil 2 baking sheets and cover with greaseproof paper. Spoon the meringue into a piping bag fitted with a 1–2 cm/½–¾ inch plain nozzle.
To form the 24 mushroom stems, pipe the meringue carefully on to 1 of the baking sheets, lifting the bag vertically until the stems are 4–5 cm/1½–2 inches high and making the base of the stem wider for support. With a small knife, carefully cut the meringue away from the nozzle. On the other baking sheet, pipe 24 even rounds of the meringue 4–5 cm/1½–2 inches in diameter and 2 cm/¾ inch thick to form the mushroom caps. Twist the bag away to prevent peaks forming.
Sift the cocoa powder over both the mushroom stems and caps. Bake in a preheated oven for 3 hours or until the meringues are dry and easily detached from the greaseproof paper. Remove from the oven and leave uncovered until cool.
When cool, use the back of a small spoon to spread a thin coating of the melted chocolate on the underneath of each mushroom cap, spreading it just to the edge. Rest the cap chocolate side up securely on an eggcup or a small glass. Place a stem, narrow end down, on to the chocolate and allow to cool until the chocolate is firmly set.
Makes 24

Clockwise from top: Dipped strawberries and crystallized ginger; Chocolate spirals; Meringue mushrooms; Chocolate creams

Chocolate spirals

Metric	Imperial
75 g unsalted butter	3 oz unsalted butter
120 g icing sugar	4 ½ oz icing sugar
1 ½ × 15 ml spoons rum	1 ½ tablespoons rum
175 g plain chocolate, melted	6 oz plain chocolate, melted

Preparation time: 20 minutes, plus setting

Beat the butter by hand in a mixing bowl until smooth and creamy. Gradually add the sugar, beating well after each addition. Continue beating until the mixture is light and fluffy. Beat in the rum.
Allow the melted chocolate to cool and thicken for about 5 minutes. Pour the chocolate into the mixing bowl and beat into the butter mixture. Continue to stir until thoroughly blended and the paste is thick and firm.
Spoon the paste into a piping bag fitted with a 1 cm/½ inch star nozzle. Line a tray with greaseproof paper and pipe the paste into spirals 3 cm/1¼ inches in diameter. Leave the spirals to harden in a cool place for a few hours.
Place the spirals in paper cases to serve.
Makes 20

Dipped strawberries

Metric	Imperial
750 g large, firm, fresh strawberries	1 ½ lb large, firm, fresh strawberries
750 g dipping or plain chocolate	1 ½ lb dipping or plain chocolate

Preparation time: 10 minutes, plus drying
Cooking time: 15–20 minutes

Choose ripe, well-coloured strawberries with their stems intact.

Wash the strawberries, leaving the stems on and pat them dry.
Using a hot but dry, heatproof bowl, melt the dipping or plain chocolate. Holding each strawberry by the stem, dip it into the chocolate, leaving the top uncovered. Allow the excess chocolate to drip off. Place the strawberries on a tray lined with non-stick silicone paper and allow them to dry.
Makes 750 g/1½ lb

Variation:
Crystallized orange peel and crystallized ginger dipped in this way are also delicious.

Chocolate tiles

Metric
50 g unsalted butter,
  softened
100 g vanilla sugar
3 egg whites
40 g plain flour
1 × 15 ml spoon cocoa
  powder
175 g flaked almonds
2 × 5 ml spoons rum

Imperial
2 oz unsalted butter,
  softened
4 oz vanilla sugar
3 egg whites
1½ oz plain flour
1 tablespoon cocoa
  powder
6 oz flaked almonds
2 teaspoons rum

Preparation time: 10 minutes
Cooking time: 5 minutes per batch
Oven: 220°C, 425°F, Gas Mark 7

These thin, crisp and delicately curved pan-tiles are an excellent accompaniment to coffee at the end of a special meal.

Beat the butter in a mixing bowl until pale and soft. Add the sugar and beat until light and fluffy. Beat in the egg whites, 1 at a time, mixing well after each addition. Sift the flour and cocoa powder together into the bowl and fold into the butter mixture, followed by 100 g/4 oz of the almonds and then the rum. Liberally butter 2 baking sheets. Spread 1 × 15 ml spoon/1 tablespoon of the batter in the shape of wide ovals as thinly as possible; use a fork dipped in cold water to help. Sprinkle each 'tile' with some of the reserved almonds.

Bake in a preheated oven for 5 minutes or until lightly crisp. When the tiles are cooked, quickly mould them over greased milk bottles, secured on their sides.
Makes about 25

Chocolate tiles; Almond crescents; Pinwheels

Almond crescents

Metric
100 g unsalted butter,
  softened
40 g caster sugar
1 egg yolk
2 × 5 ml spoons rum
150 g plain flour
1 × 15 ml spoon cocoa
  powder
50 g ground fresh
  almonds

Imperial
4 oz unsalted butter,
  softened
1½ oz caster sugar
1 egg yolk
2 teaspoons rum
5 oz plain flour
1 tablespoon cocoa
  powder
2 oz ground fresh
  almonds

To finish:
100 g plain chocolate,
  melted
150 g chopped almonds

To finish:
4 oz plain chocolate,
  melted
5 oz chopped almonds

Preparation time: 30 minutes, plus cooling
Cooking time: 20–25 minutes
Oven: 180°C, 350°F, Gas Mark 4

These light, crisp biscuits are perfect served with afternoon tea or coffee.

Beat the butter in a mixing bowl until pale and soft. Add the sugar and beat until light and fluffy. Beat in the egg yolk and rum. Sift together the flour, cocoa powder and almonds into the bowl and fold into the butter mixture. Mould walnut-sized pieces of the dough into short sausages with tapered ends. Curve into crescents and place on a buttered baking sheet.
Bake in a preheated oven for 20–25 minutes or until the crescents are firm and darker in colour. Remove to a wire tray to cool.
When cool, dip each tip into the melted chocolate and then into the chopped almonds. Place each crescent on greaseproof paper and leave until the chocolate has cooled and set.
Makes 24

Pinwheels

Metric
100 g unsalted butter,
  softened
100 g vanilla sugar
1 × 5 ml spoon grated
  lemon rind
1 egg
200 g plain flour
50 g ground walnuts
1 × 2.5 ml spoon baking
  powder
pinch of salt
1 × 15 ml spoon cocoa
  powder

Imperial
4 oz unsalted butter,
  softened
4 oz vanilla sugar
1 teaspoon grated lemon
  rind
1 egg
7 oz plain flour
2 oz ground walnuts
½ teaspoon baking
  powder
pinch of salt
1 tablespoon cocoa
  powder

Preparation time: 20 minutes, plus chilling
Cooking time: 8–10 minutes
Oven: 200°C, 400°F, Gas Mark 6

Pinwheels are alternating spirals of colour that are as much fun to make as they are to eat.

Beat the butter in a mixing bowl until pale and soft. Add the sugar and lemon rind and beat until light and fluffy. Beat in the egg. Sift together the flour, walnuts, baking powder and salt into the bowl and fold into the butter mixture. Halve the dough and set one half aside. Sift the cocoa powder into the bowl with the remaining dough and mix well. Wrap each half of dough in greaseproof paper and chill for 1 hour or until firm enough to roll.
Roll out each half of the dough into rectangles of equal size 5 mm/¼ inch thick. Place one rectangle on top of the other and press gently to secure the dough. Trim away any uneven sides and roll up the dough lengthwise like a Swiss roll. Wrap the roll in greaseproof paper and chill for 2 hours or until firm enough to slice.
Cut the dough into slices 8 mm/⅓ inch thick and place on buttered baking sheets. Bake in a preheated oven for 8–10 minutes, until the edges go crisp. Remove to a wire tray to cool.
Makes 30

Chocolate orange creams

Metric	Imperial
100 g unsalted butter, softened	4 oz unsalted butter, softened
100 g soft light brown sugar	4 oz soft light brown sugar
2 × 5 ml spoons golden syrup	2 teaspoons golden syrup
1 egg yolk	1 egg yolk
grated rind of 1 orange	grated rind of 1 orange
175 g plain flour	6 oz plain flour
1 × 15 ml spoon cocoa powder	1 tablespoon cocoa powder
1 × 2.5 ml spoon cream of tartar	½ teaspoon cream of tartar
1 × 5 ml spoon baking powder	1 teaspoon baking powder

Filling:

50 g unsalted butter, softened	2 oz unsalted butter, softened
75 g icing sugar	3 oz icing sugar
2 × 5 ml spoons orange-flavoured liqueur	2 teaspoons orange-flavoured liqueur

Preparation time: 30 minutes, plus cooling
Cooking time: 15–20 minutes
Oven: 190°C, 375°F, Gas Mark 5

A tasty and attractive sandwich biscuit, in which the orange-liqueur filling provides a sharp contrast to the chocolate-flavoured biscuit.

Beat the butter in a mixing bowl until pale and soft. Add the sugar and beat until light and fluffy. Beat in the syrup, egg yolk and orange rind. Sift the flour, cocoa powder, cream of tartar and baking powder into the bowl and fold into the butter mixture.
Shape the dough into 36 balls about the size of small walnuts and place them 4 cm/1½ inches apart, on 2 buttered baking sheets. Bake in a preheated oven for 15–20 minutes. Remove to a wire tray to cool.
Meanwhile, prepare the filling. Beat the butter in a mixing bowl until pale and soft. Gradually, in 2 or 3 additions, sift the icing sugar into the bowl, beating well after each addition. Beat in the orange-flavoured liqueur. Spread the filling evenly over half the biscuits and sandwich together with the remaining biscuits.
Makes 18

Chocolate syrup brownies

Metric	Imperial
100 g sugar	4 oz sugar
150 ml water	¼ pint water
25 g cocoa powder	1 oz cocoa powder
100 g unsalted butter	4 oz unsalted butter
225 g soft brown sugar	8 oz soft brown sugar
2 egg yolks	2 egg yolks
175 g plain flour	6 oz plain flour
1 × 1.25 ml spoon bicarbonate of soda	¼ teaspoon bicarbonate of soda
pinch of salt	pinch of salt
50–75 g chopped walnuts	2–3 oz chopped walnuts

Preparation time: 20 minutes
Cooking time: about 50 minutes
Oven: 180°C, 350°F, Gas Mark 4

Traditionally an American recipe, brownies are rich and moist. The chocolate syrup used here gives the biscuits a fudge-like consistency.

Dissolve the sugar with the water in a heavy saucepan, stirring constantly over a medium heat. Bring to the boil and cook the syrup to 102°C/215°F, or until the syrup spins a short, fine thread from a spoon. Remove the pan from the heat and add the cocoa powder. Stir until well mixed over a low heat for 2 minutes. Leave to cool.
Butter a 23 × 23 cm/9 × 9 inch cake tin and dust with flour. Beat the butter in a mixing bowl, until pale and soft. Add the sugar and continue beating until the mixture is light. Beat in the egg yolks, 1 at a time, beating well after each addition. Stir in the chocolate syrup. Sift the flour, bicarbonate of soda and salt together into the bowl and gently fold into the chocolate mixture, then stir in the chopped walnuts. Spoon into the tin and bake in a preheated oven for 40 minutes or until a skewer inserted into the centre comes out clean.
Remove to a wire tray and allow to cool slightly, then cut into squares while still warm.
Makes 16

From the front: Chocolate syrup brownies; Cocoa wafers; Chocolate orange creams

Cocoa wafers

Metric
100 g unsalted butter,
  softened
175 g sugar
1 egg yolk
1 × 15 ml spoon strong
  black coffee
50 g cocoa powder
100 g plain flour
1 × 5 ml spoon baking
  powder
pinch of salt

Imperial
4 oz unsalted butter,
  softened
6 oz sugar
1 egg yolk
1 tablespoon strong
  black coffee
2 oz cocoa powder
4 oz plain flour
1 teaspoon baking
  powder
pinch of salt

Preparation time: 15 minutes, plus chilling
Cooking time: 8–10 minutes per batch
Oven: 200°C, 400°F, Gas Mark 6

Beat the butter in a mixing bowl until pale and soft.
Add 150 g/5 oz of the sugar and beat together until
light and fluffy. Beat in the egg yolk and coffee and
mix well. Sift the cocoa powder, flour, baking powder
and salt together into the bowl and mix into the butter
mixture until just incorporated. Shape the dough into
a roll 6 cm/2½ inches in diameter. Wrap the roll in
greaseproof paper and chill for 2 hours or until firm.
Cut the dough into slices about 3 mm/⅛ inch thick
and place on ungreased baking sheets. Lightly
sprinkle each 'wafer' with some of the remaining
sugar, pressing it gently into the dough. Bake in a
preheated oven for 6–8 minutes, until the outside just
darkens. Remove to a wire tray to cool.
Makes about 40

INDEX

Dipping chocolate is available from:

Baker Smith
65 The Street
Tongham
Farnham
Surrey GU10 1DD